#17 Jefferson - Vassie D.
Wright Memorial Branch Library
2211 W. Jefferson Boulevard
Los Angeles, CA 90018

JUL 19 2017

W9-BGO-611

ONE CUT

Simon True: Real Stories. Real Teens. Real Consequences.

Also in the series:

Deep Water by Katherine Nichols

17 JEFFERSON

AUG 1 6 2017

Simon True

ONE CUT

EVE PORINCHAK

SIMON PULSE

NEW YORK LONDON TORONTO SYDNEY NEW DELHI

230890239

YOUNG ADULT
364.9794 P836

SIMON PULSE

An imprint of Simon & Schuster Children's Publishing Division

1230 Avenue of the Americas, New York, New York 10020

First Simon Pulse edition May 2017

Text copyright © 2017 by Eve Porinchak

Front cover photograph of knife copyright © 2017 by EmBaSy/Thinkstock

Back jacket photograph of knife (hardcover only) copyright © 2017 by PeterPal/Thinkstock

Cover images of spray paint copyright © 2017 by johnjohnson13/Thinkstock

All rights reserved, including the right of reproduction in whole or in part in any form.

SIMON PULSE and colophon are registered trademarks of Simon & Schuster, Inc.

For information about special discounts for bulk purchases, please contact

Simon & Schuster Special Sales at 1-866-506-1949 or business@simonandschuster.com.

The Simon & Schuster Speakers Bureau can bring authors to your live event. For more information
or to book an event contact the Simon & Schuster Speakers Bureau at 1-866-248-3049 or visit our
website at www.simonspeakers.com.

Cover designed by Sarah Creech

Interior designed by Greg Stadnyk

The text of this book was set in Chaparral Pro.

Manufactured in the United States of America

2 4 6 8 10 9 7 5 3 1

This book has been cataloged with the Library of Congress.

ISBN 978-1-4814-8132-8 (hc)

ISBN 978-1-4814-8131-1 (pbk)

ISBN 978-1-4814-8133-5 (eBook)

For my favorite person in the world—my sister, Amy—the bright light at the end of a dark tunnel for those who are given unjust sentences or are wrongfully accused. Thank you for dedicating your entire life to providing a voice for the disadvantaged. I could never have written this story—or gotten through life, for that matter—without you.

WHO'S WHO

VICTIMS

James "Jimmy" Farris: homicide victim, sixteen years old

Michael McLoren: best friend of Jimmy Farris, owner of "the Fort," seventeen years old

DEFENDANTS

Jason Holland: eighteen years old

Micah Holland: Jason Holland's brother, fifteen years old

Brandon Hein: eighteen years old

Tony Miliotti: seventeen years old

Christopher Velardo: seventeen years old

FAMILY

Nancy McLoren: mother of Michael McLoren

Georgette Thille: grandmother of Michael McLoren

Sharry Holland: mother of Jason and Micah Holland

Gary Holland: stepfather of Jason and Micah Holland

Judie Farris: mother of Jimmy Farris

Jim Farris Senior: father of Jimmy Farris

Gene Hein: father of Brandon Hein

FRIENDS/WITNESSES

Stacey Williams: girlfriend of Michael McLoren

Natasha Sinkinson: girlfriend of Christopher Velardo

Johnny Vinnedge: friend of victims

John Berardis: friend of victims

Jason Stout: friend of defendants

Dwayne Dahlberg: friend of defendants

ADDITIONAL WITNESSES

Alyce Moulder: victim of wallet theft

Phyllis Deikel: next-door neighbor to the Hein family

Barbara Wampler: next-door neighbor to the McLoren family

POLICE OFFICERS

Officer Robert Tauson: homicide detective, chief investigating officer, Los Angeles County Sheriff's Department

Officer William Neumann: homicide detective, Los Angeles County Sheriff's Department

LEGAL

Lawrence Mira: Malibu Superior Court judge

Jeffrey Semow: prosecutor, Los Angeles District Attorney's Office

Michael Latin: prosecutor, Los Angeles District Attorney's Office

Ira Salzman: defense attorney for Jason Holland

Jill Lansing: defense attorney for Brandon Hein

John Franklin: juvenile defense attorney for Micah Holland

Jim Sussman: trial attorney for Micah Holland

Curtis Leftwich: defense attorney for Tony Miliotti

Bruce Jones: juvenile defense attorney for Christopher Velardo

Charles English: adult defense attorney for Christopher Velardo

MEDIA

Mary Pols: *Los Angeles Times* newspaper reporter

Randall Sullivan: *Rolling Stone* magazine reporter

William Gazecki: documentary filmmaker of *Reckless Indifference*

THE ATTACK

"THIS IS INTERESTING," MIKE MCLOREN SAID, PEELING off his boxing gloves. "Looks like trouble."

He and his best friend, Jimmy Farris, stood at the far end of the rustic backyard, which spanned almost an entire football field. They were wrapping up a workout session, punching the heavy Everlast bag they had hung from a horizontal branch of the eucalyptus tree that shaded a makeshift backyard fort. Mike, fuming at his girlfriend, Stacey, who had just gone home, said he needed to "work out his anger." Now four teenage boys had hopped the chain-link fence surrounding the McLoren home on Foothill Drive that Mike shared with his mother and grandparents.

The sun was just slipping below the lofty peaks surrounding sleepy Agoura Hills, California, a rural enclave of suburban Los Angeles known mostly for its popularity on journalistic lists of America's Safest Cities year after year. A slightly damp sixty-degree evening—chilly by Southern California standards—didn't deter the boys. They and dozens of their friends spent most of their free time in the refuge of Mike's fort and the McLoren backyard, rain or shine.

Mike and Jimmy had constructed the clubhouse-style fort a few years earlier using wooden planks, tarps, and Plexiglas. When they were younger, they had built a playhouse in this spot. Now that they were older, they'd needed a larger, more mature fortress that would suit their new hobbies. Thirteen by fourteen feet in size, the structure stood about seven feet in height. A talented artist, Mike had painted a massive beast on one entire side of the fort's exterior. The ape-bear-boar creature loomed before a bloodred background, drooling green goo beneath pointed tusks and scowling through bloodshot eyes. The back of the fort sported colorful spray-painted shapes and black lines reminiscent of the graffiti or "tagging" that adorned many Los Angeles inner-city freeway overpasses, less than an hour's drive away.

Best friends since age seven, Mike and Jimmy were a strange pair, according to neighbors, friends, and classmates. Although the disparity between the two boys wasn't limited to their looks, Jimmy, at five feet eleven inches and with a tanned, muscular, 175-pound physique, outshone Mike, who stood one inch shorter and thirty pounds lighter. Jimmy, who wore his sun-kissed strawberry-blond hair long and loose, appeared to have stepped out of a *Surfer* magazine photo shoot. Mike, however, sported a dark, slicked-back style that brought out the paleness of his round face, and appeared more mafioso than Southern

California suburb. In fact, they were an odd couple whose reputations, popularity, and social status often contrasted throughout the years. While Jimmy exercised religiously in preparation for the Agoura High School varsity football team tryouts, Mike spent much of his free time partying. At the time, Mike could bench-press only half of what Jimmy could. Still, Jimmy pushed Mike to work out with him at least thirty minutes per day, boxing and lifting, in order to improve his health and teach him to defend himself.

Mike and Jimmy knew the trespassers. They recognized them as fifteen-year-old Micah Holland, his eighteen-year-old brother, Jason, seventeen-year-old Tony Miliotti, and a new boy they knew only as Brandon. The Holland brothers lived close by Brandon, and the three had been inseparable during the previous year. "If my boys weren't at Brandon's house, then he was over here at our house," Sharry Holland, mother to Jason and Micah, said. They might as well have been brothers, and at first glance certainly appeared to be, with their shaved heads and handsome faces. Though three years older, and legally an adult, baby-faced Brandon looked closer to Micah's age. In fact, the two looked so similar in facial features and stature, people in the neighborhood often got them confused. Neither had filled out yet, and their scrappiness bonded them. Docile Tony, close with the Holland family since childhood, enjoyed following the crowd. Though the tall, gentle blue-eyed boy didn't speak much, his integrity and loyalty to friends and family ran deep, and behind his stoic demeanor was a kind and generous heart.

The four teens walked across the backyard and approached the fort. According to Mike, young Micah led the pack, "arms sticking out like he was trying to make himself look bigger," marching like he was on a mission. Even though he was three years younger and they attended different schools, the slight five-foot-nothing, 105-pound Micah Holland had history with the much larger Mike McLoren.

Though precisely what happened next would be heavily disputed by five of the six young men, defense lawyers, police officers, prosecutors, family members, the media, and the entire community of Agoura Hills for years afterward, one fact remains certain: On the evening of Monday, May 22, 1995, less than twenty minutes after Micah, Jason, Tony, and Brandon had approached the fort, sixteen-year-old Jimmy Farris lay splayed on the tile floor of the McLoren kitchen, feet propped up on a dining chair, in a pool of blood. Dead.

WE HAVE AN EMERGENCY

IN AGOURA HILLS, THE TIGHT-KNIT COMMUNITY THIRTY miles northwest of downtown Los Angeles, real estate brokers advertise "country living with panoramic mountain views and ocean breezes." Drive less than fifteen miles north on the serpentine Malibu Canyon Road and one rolls into the famous beach town of Malibu, which boasts more celebrity mansions per square mile than any other location in the world. Pepperdine University's grassy knolls welcome motorists with velvety grandeur just yards away from California's Pacific Coast Highway. Back in 1995, famous ocean-view locales such as Gladstone's Restaurant featured fresh Pacific Ocean fare and attracted movie stars, rock stars, rap stars, professional athletes, and anyone else with money to burn who was looking to charm the ever-present paparazzi.

Entering Agoura Hills felt like traveling back in time. In the 1920s, Agoura—called Picture City back then—was a famous, highly desired backdrop for dozens of Hollywood movies. In 1927 Paramount Studios bought 2,400 acres and created a "movie ranch," where they filmed classics, mostly Westerns. This part of "the Valley," as Californians call it, may as well have been a different planet from most of LA County. After exiting the Ventura Freeway, the 101, visitors were welcomed by a sign arching over Chesebro Road with OLD AGOURA carved into the wooden beam. It was quaint, and it hadn't changed much since it was a popular stagecoach stop.

Foothill Drive screamed vintage California, with its swaths of hundred-year-old oaks sweeping the grassy hills and palms poking up in bunches every few feet. About a dozen ranch homes dotted the narrow road. Sprawling properties, each with an acre or two of plants and wildlife, standard in this part of the state, contrasted with most Los Angeles County neighborhoods, which featured only a few square feet of grass in between concrete slabs, if they were lucky. Most residents owned horses; stables and equestrian trails lay only a few blocks away. Equine scents permeated the air when breezes floated through this eerily silent street.

Monday, May 22, 1995

7:22 p.m.

911 Operator: Hello?

Nancy McLoren (Mike McLoren's mother): Is this 911?

911 Operator: Yes.

Nancy McLoren: We have an emergency. The boys came in and they're bleeding. They were stabbed.

911 Operator: How old are they?

Nancy McLoren: Sixteen, seventeen.

911 Operator: Did you say they were stabbed?

Nancy McLoren: I guess so.

911 Operator: Okay, you need to ask them. If they were stabbed, what happened?

Nancy McLoren: This one is about to pass out. He's bleeding all over the place!

Woman's voice in the background: Send somebody!

Soon after seven p.m. that evening, the McLoren family had finished eating dinner and Mike walked outside to his backyard fort to meet up with Jimmy. Mike's mother, Nancy—a local elementary school teacher—sat down at her kitchen table to grade papers, while his grandparents retreated to the living room to watch *Jeopardy!* About fifteen minutes later, the back door swung open. Jimmy staggered into the kitchen first, collapsed onto the table, and rolled right into Nancy's arms. Mike followed. Both boys were bleeding through their shirts.

Jimmy's parents, Jim and Judie Farris, also lived on Foothill Drive, opposite the McLorens, about six houses down. Judie later reported that soon after seven p.m. she sat in her own kitchen and wondered where her son Jimmy was and why he was late. Jimmy's father, Jim Farris Senior, was working a night shift. Judie and Jimmy had a dinner date. After nearly seventeen years sharing a maternal bond with her baby boy, her youngest son, whom she described as "the closest thing to an angel on Earth that I ever knew," Judie Farris experienced what can only be defined as an extrasensory-perception or sixth-sense moment at 7:18 p.m.

"I jumped out of my chair, like someone put a tack under me. I thought, I have to get to him now."

Moments later Georgette Thille, Mike McLoren's grand-mother, phoned the Farris residence and shouted to Judie, "Jimmy's been stabbed!"

Judie ran the one hundred yards up Foothill Drive and arrived at the McLoren home within minutes. The McLorens had laid Jimmy on his back on the kitchen floor, with his feet propped up on a dining room chair. They pressed towels against his wound. Soon police and paramedics rolled up to the house. Both Jimmy and Mike were still bleeding. Jimmy had stopped breathing. Mike McLoren was immediately strapped to a stretcher, rolled to an ambulance, and rushed to a helicopter that flew him to the UCLA Medical Center. Paramedics pressed on Jimmy's chest for twenty minutes, attempting to revive him through cardiopulmo-nary resuscitation, while the blood poured from his chest. Judie Farris stood above Jimmy in the McLoren kitchen and peered into her son's open eyes. One of his feet slipped off the chair. She screamed, "Jimmy, don't die! I love you. I need you. Please don't die!" He stared straight ahead. His skin grew gray.

Judie Farris could not understand why Mike had been airlifted to safety, while her beloved son was lying in a pool of his own blood. "Put him in the ambulance!" she shouted at the authorities. What she didn't realize, and could not possibly comprehend, was that Jimmy had probably bled out within a few minutes of the stabbing. He very well may have died a minute or two before Judie received the phone call. Paramedics perform CPR only if a patient fails to breathe and lacks a pulse. At that point, the chances of coming back to life are extremely low. If a patient does not receive CPR within five to ten minutes after cardiac arrest, then arrive in a setting where doctors are equipped to restart the heart, the chances of survival are zero. By the time the paramedics arrived on the scene at the McLoren home, Jimmy had passed on. Still, the medics were ethically required to perform lifesaving measures for a reasonable length of time before surrendering to the inevitable. What began as an average sunny spring day had morphed into hell on earth for two families. Soon the nightmare would swallow up five more families.

Despite his injuries, Mike had still been talking and breathing. He had a beating heart. Paramedics knew that his wounds were probably fatal. Still, there was time to save his life if they flew him to a trauma center immediately. Just before he was wheeled away on a stretcher, he spoke with two police deputies and described what had transpired, or at least what he believed he remembered. According to Mike, just after seven p.m., he and Jimmy were exercising outside his fort. A group of four boys he knew hopped the fence and walked toward them. He did not know why they had come over, he said. He thought maybe the guys were there to steal his television and VCR. After all, he "had a lot of nice stuff inside the fort." Videocassette recorders (VCRs) preceded DVD and Blu-ray players and any type of media-streaming mechanisms. VCRs were giant electronic boxes that recorded and played movies using ten-inch rectangular videocassette tapes.

Also, according to Mike McLoren, when a "fight broke out," Jimmy jumped into the fray. Mike told deputies he thought he remembered being "stabbed by Micah Holland." Next, Jimmy was also stabbed, but Mike couldn't see who the perpetrator was. McLoren described the fight as happening very quickly. But he claimed he was certain about who was there. He named four people: Micah Holland, Jason Holland, and two other kids—a boy named Brandon and a mutual friend of all the boys, seventeen-year-old Chris Velardo.

Over the subsequent days and months, this story would change countless times.

THE ALYCE MOULDER

INCIDENT

AFTER JIMMY AND MIKE FLED THE SCENE AND stumbled into the McLoren home, Micah, Jason, Brandon, and Tony stood in or around the fort for a few seconds before gathering themselves together. The four boys walked slowly from the fort to the fence and climbed back over. A neighbor reported that he was jogging that evening around seven thirty p.m. and saw four teenage boys walking from the McLoren fence to a parked maroon truck. They appeared to be in no hurry, and he recalled that they were smiling or smirking as they climbed into the pickup truck.

Though Mike had initially told police officers that Chris Velardo was one of the four boys he had seen climb over his fence and approach the fort, Chris never actually entered the McLoren property with the others before the brawl. He had remained sitting in the driver's seat of his Nissan truck, which was parked across the street, the entire time. The tall, slim seventeen-year-old, with his chocolate eyes and wavy chestnut hair, could easily have been mistaken for a telenovela soap star. Chris watched the four boys pile back into his truck. The five friends then drove up the hill to a cul-de-sac in a small housing development. They sat on the curb, and the others filled Chris in on the fight. They had all heard Mike McLoren say, "What's up, Micah?" Then, when Micah and McLoren walked into the fort together, suddenly "fists started flying," they told Chris. Jason rushed in after his brother. Then Brandon and Jimmy followed. It was completely dark inside the fort, so nobody had seen much of anything. Everything happened within about twenty seconds. Somebody joked that McLoren must have been raging on steroids, because he had suddenly become really strong, when most of their friends had always referred to him as a "little weakling." Micah and Brandon both had cuts, scrapes, and bruises already surfacing on their faces, arms, and chests. The skin surrounding Micah's left eye started to swell.

Police officer Richard Ramirez had been patrolling the Calabasas area that evening. The mini towns of Calabasas and Agoura Hills lie adjacent to each other and often function as the same city, sharing a sprawling community center and the Lost Hills Sheriff's Station, which lies tucked among the chaparral hiking trails. Ramirez had received a call at 7:11 p.m. regarding a theft. The victim had called 911 from the parking lot of Village Market, the local liquor and convenience store in Calabasas.

Sometime between six thirty and seven p.m., local resident Alyce Moulder had been playing with her two young children at the Gates

Canyon Park playground. Built only two years earlier, the park featured tennis courts, a basketball court, and a play structure designed specifically for the needs of small children with physical disabilities. The charming park lay among rolling meadows and walking paths, isolated from the residential neighborhoods and strip malls. Still, it embodied suburban security. In this part of Los Angeles, people forget to lock their car doors; it's simply not necessary.

The distance from the playground to the cramped parking lot was a stone's throw, and Alyce watched as a maroon Nissan pickup truck full of teenagers drove into the lot. What happened next shocked her into a frenzy. One of the boys climbed out of the truck and opened the front door of her van. He snatched her wallet right off the dashboard, and then he jumped back into the bed of the truck. They sped away. Enraged, Alyce scooped up her children and loaded them into her van.

While Alyce Moulder stood in the parking lot of Village Market with Officer Ramirez, he took notes as she told him a story about how she stepped on the gas and tailed the boys in the truck all the way to the parking lot to confront them. The teens denied having her wallet. They took off again. It was then that Alyce called the police, she said. As she concluded her report to Officer Ramirez, a man ran up and handed the police officer a wallet he retrieved after he spotted it being tossed from the back of a pickup truck on Thousand Oaks Boulevard. Alyce Moulder identified the wallet as hers and combed through it. Nothing was missing. It never had any cash in it to begin with.

Later, at 8:40 that evening, Officer Ramirez saw a maroon

Nissan truck full of boys driving in the opposite direction on Thousand Oaks Boulevard. He quickly swung his squad car around and pulled the truck over. According to Officer Ramirez's report, one of the boys exited the truck, raised his hands in the air, and instantly said, "Don't freak out. I have a knife." Ramirez frisked the boy and retrieved a small folding pocketknife. The officer flipped the knife open and inspected it. It was a common and harmless tool, not to mention completely legal. It was also clean. Officer Ramirez searched the other boys. None had weapons. None seemed suspicious. They were polite and cooperative enough. He never asked for names. He handed the pocketknife back and let them go. After all, even if this was the truck full of teen boys who'd stolen Alyce Moulder's wallet, nothing had been taken out of the wallet, and the property had been returned to its rightful owner. Alyce had refused to press charges. No harm done.

Though Jimmy Farris had been dead for more than an hour, Officer Richard Ramirez knew nothing of the fight or the stabbing. He certainly had no idea that the compact folding knife he had just handed back could possibly have been the weapon used in a murder case that would soon divide and haunt this once affable community.

The Alyce Moulder Incident, as it was later labeled, would eventually morph into a massive legal nail that would be hammered into the coffins of five young men.

THE FORT

SOON AFTER TEN O'CLOCK THAT EVENING, DETECTIVE
Robert Tauson of the LA County Sheriff's Department drove out
to Foothill Drive and entered the McLorens' house. Now the lead
detective on the case, Tauson was a soft-spoken middle-aged man
with immaculate salt-and-pepper hair and a graying mustache to
match. He wore square eyeglasses that looked too large for his face.
After he was handed keys to crack open the two heavy locks protecting the door to the fort, Detective Tauson walked into the backyard and approached the structure, about seventy-five feet from
the house. Why was it locked? At that moment, Mike McLoren
lay in a hospital in serious condition. Jimmy Farris lay dead. Still,
someone had taken the time to lock up the door to the fort.

The yard and the fort interior were both pitch black. Through
the beam of his flashlight, Tauson took note of the chaos of the
one-room shack, which he described as "pretty much decorated like

a teenager's bedroom." He tripped a few times. Even after he found the light switch, the fort remained extremely dim. Three faint bulbs provided the only illumination; one was painted blue, one green. Neon posters tacked up on black walls featured butterflies, a cheetah, a zebra, and a serpent, together creating a trippy 1960s drug-den vibe. A light-green plush chair, with stuffing popping out in tufts where the fabric appeared to have been chewed away by wild dogs, rested against a wooden desk with a locked drawer. A brown leather couch sat up against one wall. A bed pressed against another. Items that could have been used as weapons lay scattered on the floor—a baseball bat, a hammer, an air rifle, and a broom. Cups, drinking glasses, tennis balls, photos, empty buckets, and food-crusted dishes were strewn throughout. To describe the fort as cramped was a massive understatement. A red plaid blanket hung up on the wall covered the only Plexiglas window.

Lengthy ropes of extension cords twisted around the floor. The fort had its own electric power and phone lines that ran from the main house. This was an era before cell phones and streaming. The term "wireless" did not exist. The television and VCR that Mike had mentioned to the first deputies on the scene sat undisturbed on a shelf. They were both pretty dusty. In fact, the only signs Detective Tauson reported seeing that indicated there might have been a struggle included an upside-down plastic lawn chair and a pile of sheets that might have been grabbed off the now stripped bed. The baseball bat on the floor appeared to have a small amount of blood on it.

Tauson unlocked the desk drawer. Photos tacked to the wall

above featured marijuana buds shimmering with crystal-like beads. Inside the drawer he discovered just less than twenty dollars in cash and five small plastic bags filled with marijuana. The irony was a bit disturbing. Not only was murder a complete rarity in Agoura Hills, but this town was the top choice for Southern California law enforcement professionals to settle down. Police officers and their families flocked to this area because drugs and crime were never a problem here like they were in urban Los Angeles. In fact, just a few months earlier, the *Los Angeles Times* had run a story that rated Agoura as the safest of all the communities in the Conejo Valley, exhibiting the lowest number of incidents for various crimes. Foothill Drive was full of nice homes, churchgoing families, stay-at-home moms, and kids who played sports. This wasn't the hood, where residents dodged bullets while walking to the grocery store. And it certainly wasn't a street where drug deals went down. Or was it?

The Jimmy Farris murder would quickly erode the veneer of safety and family values that the community had enjoyed for so long. Not only did the murder thrust fear and panic into the once carefree culture, but it turned neighbor against neighbor and forced parents to rethink their levels of trust in their seemingly flawless children.

Although he could not have foreseen the profound implications of what was on his mind that night, one thought must certainly have plagued Detective Tauson while he rummaged through Mike McLoren's fort.

These boys didn't just kill a kid. They killed the youngest son of a beloved Los Angeles Police Department homicide detective.

YOU'RE WANTED FOR
MURDER

AROUND THE SAME TIME DETECTIVE ROBERT TAUSON was investigating the crime scene inside the fort, Sharry Holland sat in her apartment, waiting for her youngest son, Micah, to return home for the night. A stunning forty-year-old southern belle, Sharry was a straight shooter with a smooth Louisiana twang. The single mother worked long hours selling real estate, and she trusted her boys with the freedom she gave them. She knew they liked to party and have fun. Still, she had always figured it was a normal part of adolescence that "they'd eventually grow out of, like everybody does." Sharry was the one parent whom Jason and Micah's friends could count on. She listened, she was honest and nonjudgmental, and they never felt like they had to lie to her. Most days she knew exactly what they were all up to. Again, she trusted that they'd never get into serious trouble. And if they did, her boys were smart enough to know how serious the consequences could be.

Micah had called earlier, drunk, from a nearby McDonald's. Sharry demanded he come straight home. Neither Jason nor Brandon attended school anymore. Both now eighteen years old, they had quit high school, forgoing graduation. Jason had just taken and passed the GED days before. Therefore, staying out late on a weeknight didn't much matter. Micah, however, was only fifteen and couldn't afford any more trouble with the law. He had racked up four blemishes on his juvenile record since age ten and was lucky to have avoided jail time.

After being searched and released by Officer Ramirez, Micah, Jason, Brandon, Tony, and Chris had hopped back into the Nissan truck around nine p.m. and driven down Thousand Oaks Boulevard to a nearby McDonald's restaurant. Fairly certain that nobody who had been in McLoren's fort could possibly have been harmed—after all, the fight had lasted less than a minute and everybody walked out alive—the boys ordered and ate cheese-burgers, completely oblivious to their impending doom. Little did they know that those delicious concoctions of beef, grease, pickles, and ketchup/mustard sauce were the last they would enjoy for years, if not forever. Worse, it was the last meal the friends would ever share.

Chris Velardo drove Brandon Hein home to the condominium in Oak Park that he shared with his father, Gene Hein, and Gene's fiancée, Janice. Micah Holland ignored his mother's request that he return home and instead decided to spend the night at Brandon's house. Tony Miliotti was driven back to the home in West Hills where he lived with his aunt and uncle. And Jason was

19

driven to his friend Dwayne Dahlberg's house. He stayed there chatting for a bit, then walked down to their other friend Jason Stout's house, where he planned to spend the night.

While Sharry lay awake, anticipating Micah's return, somebody pounded on her front door. She opened it. Suddenly, five sheriff's deputies clad in uniforms, wielding guns, sprang toward her. The men pushed into her apartment.

"What's wrong? What's wrong?" Sharry asked again and again.

The officers initially hesitated in answering. Panting and waving guns, they repeatedly asked where Jason and Micah were, and whom they were with. Finally they broke the news: "Jason and Micah are wanted for murder." They explained that Jimmy Farris had been killed earlier in the evening and that both of her sons may have been involved.

After the deputies instructed Sharry to call them as soon as she located her sons, they drove away. Micah called home again. He told his mother he would be staying the night with Brandon. Imagine the level of angst Sharry Holland must have felt in that moment. "I couldn't see encouraging the boys to run," she later said. She also could not fathom that either of her sons, or their friends, could have been involved in a murder. "I figured, at worst . . . maybe they knew somebody that did this." Sharry did not tell Micah that he was wanted for murder. She did give him permission to stay at Brandon's house but insisted they stay in for the night. Next, she did the only thing she could. She dialed the number the sheriff's deputies had given her and informed them that Micah had just called her from the Hein residence on Sunnycrest Drive.

At midnight the phone rang again. It was Jason calling from Jason Stout's bedroom phone.

"You better come home," his mother said. "The police came here."

"Why?"

"Jason, Jimmy Farris is dead."

"No way."

"You're wanted for murder!" Sharry Holland shouted the four words that would transform their lives from that point forward.

Anxiety washed over Jason in that moment. "Good-bye, Mom," he said to his distraught mother. "I love you. I love you. I love you." He hung up the phone, walked out of the bedroom toward the front door, and told Jason Stout he couldn't stay the night. As he grabbed the doorknob to leave, the two boys looked out the front window and saw headlights of a car rolling into the Stouts' driveway.

After looking carefully at the front grille and coloring of the car, Jason Stout said, "Is that a police car?"

Jason's panic intensified exponentially. He made a quick decision. Without saying another word to his friend, Jason Holland sprinted across the room and out the back door. He then climbed over the backyard fence, and vanished into the night.

LOST HILLS

IN THE EARLY-MORNING HOURS OF TUESDAY, MAY 23, sheriff's deputies charged into Gene Hein's home. They apprehended and handcuffed Brandon, who was sitting awake in the living room with his father. They hustled up the stairs and found Micah snuggled in a sleeping bag. He was woken up and cuffed as well. The boys were read their rights. Specifically, the "right to remain silent" stood out. Gene Hein told Brandon not to say a word until he could get down to the station with an attorney. The boys were informed they were being arrested for a murder, then whisked away to the Lost Hills Sheriff's Station.

Detective William Neumann, Officer Robert Tauson's partner, took note of the boys' condition. Both Micah and Brandon appeared battered. Micah's left eye was swollen, and deep scratches ran down the left side of his neck and chest.

Brandon's right arm and hand displayed large scrapes or cuts, and his left shoulder was bruised. When Officer Neumann requested interviews, Brandon refused to speak, as he'd been told. His father was in the process of calling around to friends, trying to find someone who could quickly locate a criminal lawyer. However, at the request of his mother, Micah spoke. His voice shook and revealed that he had yet to reach puberty.

Tuesday, May 23, 1995

Lost Hills Sheriff's Station

3:00 a.m.

Detective Neumann: Okay, I noticed you have some puffiness and, uh, your eye is slightly bruised. Did you get hit in the eye?

Micah: I don't know. I can't remember.

Detective Neumann: Were you guys angry when you went over there?

Micah: No . . . we were angry after we started fighting. It was a quick fight. It was like ten seconds. And then he ran into the house . . . and we left.

Micah emphasized the word *ten*, as if to imply that nothing bad—certainly not a murder—could have occurred in such a short span of time.

Micah: Am I going to be charged with murder?

Detective Neumann: Yes.

Micah: I am??

Detective Neumann: Yeah, we told you from the very beginning that you were charged with murder.

Micah: I didn't know any of this happened. I didn't do anything. And I just want to go home . . .

That last word *home* expanded a few extra beats as he spoke, his tone soft and pleading, then trailing off. The fear must have clutched him right then like a massive vise squeezing his body. In that moment, did Micah definitively grasp the notion that he might never see his home again? When the detectives explained that Jimmy had been stabbed with a knife, Micah remained emphatic. "I didn't have a knife. I know that. And I know Brandon didn't have a knife. And I'm pretty positive my brother didn't. I'm almost sure." Micah explained to Detectives Tauson and Neumann that he'd simply asked Mike McLoren for some marijuana, "and he started, like, yellin' at me. And all of a sudden, just all these people swinging."

When asked why he thought Mike was so angry, Micah said, "I guess he thought I was, like—I don't know—gonna take it or something," referring to the pot he had asked to smoke. Though the above statement seemed like a reasonable inference and harmless at the time, the fate of all the boys involved in the Monday-evening fight later hinged on the truth behind those three words, *gonna take it.*

The truth of the matter was that smoking pot in Mike McLoren's fort was not only common, but it was the most popular place to smoke marijuana in all of Agoura Hills. Only three blocks from Agoura High School, the fort was the after-school pilgrimage destination for many of Mike and Jimmy's classmates. There was always a crowd, and friends enjoyed the bong closet with an assortment of pipes and a steady supply of alcohol. Most of Mike's friends and acquaintances later reported to police that he regularly gave the pot away, or smoked with them.

Back in 1995, the possession and selling of marijuana was highly illegal. The "Just Say No" and D.A.R.E. to Keep Kids Off Drugs campaigns of the 1980s kicked off massive overhauls in American schools, infiltrating the curriculum as part of President Reagan's war on drugs. Labeled a "gateway drug," marijuana was the alleged culprit of most drug addictions. Even if there was no scientific evidence to support that marijuana was addictive, it was considered a major enemy in the drug war. The assumption was that if kids smoked pot, they would inevitably move on to harder, more damaging drugs like cocaine and heroin. The medicinal and therapeutic effects of marijuana were largely ignored at that time in American history.

Micah and Brandon were held in separate cells at the Lost Hills Sheriff's Station for the next day or so. According to Micah, he was so exhausted after a day of partying, being interrogated, and no sleep that the entire experience became a blur. Though he could hardly keep his eyes open or his body upright, Micah was rattled and jarred awake every time he dozed by the banging of steel doors and the constant booming voice of the police intercom.

By Tuesday afternoon the shocking news had broken in the community. At nine o'clock the previous night, Jimmy Farris had been declared dead at Westlake Medical Center, the result of a stab wound. Mike McLoren was admitted to the UCLA Medical Center suffering from a lacerated liver and a collapsed lung. James Christianson, principal of Agoura High School, where both Mike and Jimmy were sophomores, announced the news to his two thousand students. Emergency crisis counseling immediately went into effect. Flower bunches and ribbons were stuffed into the chain-link fence surrounding the McLoren home. Neon yellow CAUTION tape circled the fort.

Sharry Holland issued a statement on the evening news expressing deep sympathy for the Farris family. She also stated her undying love for her sons and pleaded with Jason to surrender. Acknowledging that he must be "scared, severely depressed, and tired," she reiterated her hope that her eldest son would do the right thing. "I have not heard from him, nor do I know where he is."

The notion that this idyllic community harbored a secret sinister element spread quickly. The fact that Jimmy Farris was popular and well liked made it feel even more frightening. Classmates remembered him as "proud to be an American." He was described as "nice and innocent," and "a well-mannered kid, who would take off his shirt for anyone." Neighbors spoke to *Los Angeles Times* reporters and expressed concern that "there's no place to run anymore." One mother explained that she had moved to Agoura Hills from West Los Angeles two years before to avoid the gang violence that had just started erupting on the west side of the city. The Valley was supposed to offer refuge from that type of violence.

After a couple of days, Micah Holland was transferred and locked up in the Barry J. Nidorf juvenile detention facility in Sylmar, California. Brandon Hein was being held at the Los Angeles County Men's Central Jail. The downtown facility was old and dilapidated, smelled of feces and urine, and was over-crowded with mostly gangbangers. Brandon was lucky that his attorney had secured a private cell for him because of his age and lack of a violent record.

Once pieces of news leaked out, Chris Velardo gathered his family members, armed himself with defense attorney Bruce Jones, and turned himself in to the Lost Hills Sheriff's Station. Because he was still a minor, Chris was also sent to the Sylmar juvenile facility. All three boys were booked on charges of rob-bery, attempted murder, and murder.

THE GUMBYS AND THE GREMLINS

ON THE AFTERNOON OF THURSDAY, MAY 25, pathologists performed an autopsy on Jimmy Farris. He had two superficial knife stab wounds to the front of his torso. One wound on the left side of the body measured less than two inches deep. However, the blade had slid through the intercostal muscles sandwiched between two ribs, and just nicked the pericardial sac that surrounds the heart. Jimmy bled out within minutes. Had the knife landed a few centimeters to the side, he would have lived.

Also on Thursday, headlines splashed across California newspapers broadcasted the "possibly gang-related" murder of an LAPD officer's son, a story angle that seemed to have developed out of nowhere. Gang activity hadn't been synonymous with the Valley since the days of the Old West. Two juveniles and one eighteen-year-old adult were in custody. Another juvenile (Tony

Miliotti) was wanted for questioning. And one eighteen-year-old fugitive was still on the loose and possibly dangerous, the papers reported. Intimate friends and family of Jason, Micah, Brandon, Chris, and Tony were shocked. Though the boys had been involved in light scrapes with the law—truancy, fights, and other typical teenage offenses—nobody who spoke with police or reporters could comprehend that the boys were involved in gang activity, let alone murder.

As the community grasped for a reasonable explanation and motive, the media circulated two rumors. Seventeen-year-old Scott DeGeorge, a longtime friend of Mike McLoren's, told *Los Angeles Times* reporters that "a group of teenagers" had recently been breaking into the fort and stealing things. He never identified who they were. DeGeorge said he believed that on Monday, McLoren had somehow retrieved the stolen items. Then the group must have come looking for Mike, in order to take back what they had previously stolen.

Stacey Williams, Mike McLoren's girlfriend, who had left the fort just minutes before the fight, had a more ominous theory. Stacey told police officers that the stabbing was most likely payback for Mike having snitched on another friend. A little more than two years earlier, Mike—then only fourteen years old—had been arrested for stealing a police officer's gun from a family home. When he learned he would face charges, Mike fingered his crime partner, a very popular eighteen-year-old friend. Mutual friend John Berardis corroborated this last part of the story and stated that "within a week" of Mike's 1993 arrest and informing on his friend, "everyone wanted him dead." Though Mike McLoren was still a minor, his friend faced adult prison time for the crime. Further, according to Stacey, this adult friend was allegedly a member of the Gumbys.

The Gumbys were upper-middle-class Caucasian wannabe gang members. Originally a small group of friends from North Hollywood, the Gumbys had allegedly spread to the Valley. The year 1995 was sort of a heyday for Los Angeles street gangs. Although more than twenty years had passed since fifteen-year-old Raymond Lee Washington began organizing the infamous Crips gang, the 1990s witnessed a surge of street gang worship. Rap and hip-hop moguls like Dr. Dre, Snoop Dogg, and Tupac Shakur were launching massive careers and becoming recognizable to mainstream audiences, while still paying homage to their violent upbringings on gang-infested streets. Suburban wannabe gangs, trying to emulate the lifestyles of authentic hard-core gangsters, popped up in safe communities all over the country. Still, according to the Los Angeles Sheriff's Department, the worst thing the Gumbys ever did was spray-paint a couple of freeway overpasses with their gang moniker. The LAPD Gang and Narcotics Division failed to recognize them as a real threat. They were never on any watch lists. A violent, organized crime conglomerate they were not.

The main problem with this speculation from the community and the media was that nothing was proven yet. There was still no solid evidence to create a story about what had actually gone down that night in the fort. Still, between Scott DeGeorge's tale about "burglars" snatching Mike McLoren's valuables, and the news outlets clinging to a snazzy gang theory, the general public was already making up its mind. The court of public opinion was prematurely convicting the group of five teens of robbery, gang activity, and murder. They were, in effect, guilty until proven innocent.

On Thursday, May 25, Brandon Hein pled not guilty to charges of murder, attempted murder, and robbery during his arraignment. His father, Gene, had retained defense attorney Jill Lansing, who had recently enjoyed a lot of positive international press for her defense skills. Lansing was a young, thin, poised attorney who, in January 1994, had successfully defended twenty-six-year-old Lyle Menendez in what was then considered the murder trial of the century. In 1989 twenty-one-year-old Lyle and his eighteen-year-old brother, Erik, had gunned down their wealthy parents in their Beverly Hills mansion one warm summer evening, in an alleged attempt to inherit millions of dollars. The murder trial became an international media circus, as this was the first time television cameras had been allowed inside an American courtroom. Court TV cut its teeth on the Menendez murder trial, and reality television as we now know it was born.

The Menendez trial ended with two deadlocked juries, who could not decide whether to acquit or convict the boys. Although Lyle and Erik were tried together, two juries were assigned—one for each brother—because it was suggested that they may have had different levels of culpability (meaning one brother forced the other to shoot) and there were pieces of evidence that attorneys wanted only one jury to hear and not the other. The boys were tried together in an attempt to provide them their due process in a cost-efficient manner. Murder trials are expensive, and holding two that would be mostly identical seemed like an enormous waste of taxpayers' money.

The conclusion of this six-month trial was considered a major loss for the Los Angeles district attorney's office and beyond embarrassing. Here were two athletic, wealthy young men who had methodically planned out the mob-style execution of their parents, then immediately enjoyed a spending spree where they purchased a Porsche, Rolex watches, and a restaurant/bar, all before their parents were even buried. After the second jury announced its inability to agree on a conviction, District Attorney Gil Garcetti wasted no time expressing his frustration with the outcome and announcing his intention to retry the case all over again, with no room for any plea bargains. "We have an ethical, professional, moral responsibility to go forward with this case as a first-degree murder case," he said. "This may cost $1 million. We are seeking justice and that is what we are going to do, and be damned with how much money it is going to cost."

The Menendez brothers claimed they'd feared for their lives. They insisted their parents had been abusive. They claimed self-defense, even though they had ambushed their parents from behind at ten o'clock on a Sunday evening as the two watched a movie and ate ice cream with strawberries. Erik and Lyle Menendez shot both Kitty and José multiple times, reloaded their Mossberg

12-gauge shotguns, and continued shooting as José lay dead and Kitty scrambled to crawl away. The premeditation could not have been more apparent. Although the crime was brutal and Lyle Menendez even admitted to plotting and executing the murder, the jury members still felt sorry for him. There was no doubt Jill Lansing had earned that international fame and praise. She had some serious skills when it came to gaining sympathy from a jury. And now she would be in Brandon Hein's corner.

At the same time Brandon was pleading not guilty, thousands of households across the country were reading the *Los Angeles Times* morning newspaper. When the *Times* article talked a little about the background of all the boys involved, they clearly separated the victims from the perpetrators. The article explained that Jimmy and Mike attended Agoura High School, while Brandon and Micah had been transferred to Oak View, the continuation school, which was provided as an alternative to the traditional high school for teens who were at a high risk for not graduating on time. Jason had attended Indian Hills, also a continuation school, for a short while, before dropping out when he turned eighteen. At the time, many continuation schools had reputations as warehouses for the troubled youth that had been kicked out of conventional high schools.

The *Times* reporters interviewed one former classmate, who described the trio of Jason, Micah, and Brandon as "trouble-makers." Then she added, "They always have knives on them." She didn't elaborate.

"They were just kind of bullies," an eighth grader said, "just to be popular and show that they rule."

Detective Bill Neumann also gave an interview. He made a lot of assumptions. He said the four teenagers, three in custody and one on the run, were members of a gang called the Gremlins. Neumann said, definitively, that these four "gang members" had repeatedly stolen stereo and electronic equipment from Mike McLoren in the past. Last Monday, they had "broken into Mike McLoren's fort" and "attacked Mike McLoren and Jimmy Farris." So now the boys were connected to two different gangs, the Gumbys—named after the main character in a sweet 1950s animated Claymation TV show, who spread kindness and cheer throughout the world, and the Gremlins—named after a 1984 Steven Spielberg film featuring furry, monkeylike creatures who unleash hilarious chaos into their perfectly sedate community.

The funny part was that Gremlins was a joke name created by Dave Wiley, a mutual friend of all seven boys. Wiley, like the others, enjoyed partying in his free time. Because the Agoura Hills boys liked to have house parties that often got out of hand in terms of the messes they created, bottles strewn about, torn paintings, and broken household knickknacks, Dave Wiley liked to joke that he and his friends were like Gremlins. In the film, the Gremlins go crazy, becoming hyperactive and destructive when they get wet. So the joke was, add liquid and all hell breaks loose.

Then Detective Neumann made an unexpected announcement. The LA County Sheriff's Department was submitting a request to the district attorney's office. The department requested that the two juveniles, fifteen-year-old Micah Holland and seventeen-year-old Chris Velardo, face trials as adults for the murder of Jimmy Farris. If the juvenile court agreed to try them as adults, the implication was that the crime was so heinous that the ages of the defendants should be disregarded. Further, being tried as an adult for murder carried a potential sentence of life in prison.

SUPER-PREDATORS

IN THE EARLY 1990S, POLITICAL SCIENTIST AND criminologist John Dilulio described a brand-new crop of youth popping up all over the country, like a deadly virus sweeping the nation. After visiting prisons and juvenile facilities and gathering data for about ten years, he coined the term *super-predator*, which immediately became the psychobabble criminal justice buzzword of the decade. Dilulio visited the White House to consult with President Bill Clinton, and he wrote a now-famous article for the *Weekly Standard* magazine called "The Coming of the Super-Predators." Dilulio stated that after conducting years of exhaustive research, he'd concluded that America was sitting on top of a giant crime bomb that was ticking away, just waiting to explode and overflow into not just the inner cities, but the peaceful suburbs and rural towns as well.

A self-described tough guy with a linebacker's build and a

rough-streets upbringing, John Dilulio said that during his research he was always on high alert when visiting maximum-security prisons filled with "killers, rapists, and muggers." Still, nothing frightened him more than visiting the juvenile lockup facilities spread across America, all filled with "vacant stares and smiles, and remorseless eyes." He cited a study conducted in 1993 showing that kids and teens were beginning to travel in "homicidal wolf packs," where one-third of the time their victims were strangers.

The real problem in America? Moral poverty. These kids, primarily males, were "fatherless, jobless, and godless," he said. Dilulio and his colleagues predicted that this bloodbath of violent events caused by youth would triple its rate by 2005. They had studies and statistics to prove it. Not only that, but the violence itself would snowball, meaning that previous offenders would become increasingly violent if left out on the streets.

Television and other news outlets jumped on the bandwagon of this war against troubled children and were relentless in perpetuating the moral panic. The first lines of a May 1996 *Tampa Tribune* article read, "They are called super-predators. They are predicted to be a plague upon the United States in the next decade. They are not some creature from outer space; they are our own children."

Dilulio advised President Clinton, and the world, to take heed and start locking up these cold-blooded, ugly, dangerous children quickly. His suggestion that the numbers of these predators roaming the streets was about to rise exponentially over the coming decades had a profound impact on juvenile justice policy. This coming tidal wave of unprecedented youth violence needed to be stopped. Cage these vicious, broken kids now! The implication was that this new breed of teen was unsalvageable. Dilulio's warnings triggered a massive political movement in juvenile justice. The focus, he said, needed to steer away from rehabilitation (which had historically been its foundation) and toward punishment and removal from society.

The Violent Youth Predator Act of 1996 offered $1.5 billion in grant monies to states that chose to toughen their juvenile offender laws. Forty-five states quickly changed their laws dealing with juvenile offenders. Most of America completely overhauled legislation that the public deemed too lax. Newt Gingrich, Speaker of the House of Representatives at the time, stated, "There are no violent offenses that are juvenile. You rape somebody, you are an adult. You shoot somebody, you are an adult." Senator and presidential candidate Bob Dole later added, "Kids that once stole hubcaps now rape and murder. No fear of punishment. Experts call them super-predators."

In many states, children as young as thirteen could be tried as adults, and therefore receive sentences formerly reserved for adults. Also, this meant that some children under age eighteen would serve their time in adult facilities, depending on the state and the crime. According to the Justice Policy Institute in Washington, DC, youth incarcerated with adults are five times more likely to suffer sexual assaults, twice as likely to be beaten by prison staff, and fifty times more likely to be attacked with a weapon than youth who remain in juvenile facilities.

The irony in all of this? Two decades later, John Dilulio realized that his assumptions and calculations had been dead wrong. Instead of youth crime tripling, it was literally cut in half. In fact, at the time he made his predictions, violent youth crime had been plummeting for a while. After the 1980s, the economy was improving drastically, there were major drops in crack cocaine usage around the country, and impoverished areas were on the upswing. The tsunami never arrived. It hadn't ever begun. Dilulio fully admitted that he'd inadvertently created a myth, a hype that led to fear that led to major changes in too many laws that stuck indefinitely. Eventually, he completely lost faith in predictions based on social science. "Criminology is not a pure science," he says.

John Dilulio now advocates for youth offenders and lobbies to cut their life sentences. After much analysis, he firmly believes that his mistaken prediction paved the way for treatment of children that is cruel and unusual. Unfortunately for Jason, Brandon, Micah, Chris, and Tony, the invention of the super-predator could not have come at a worse time.

THE INTERVIEW

Friday, May 26, 1995, Morning

UCLA Medical Center

Detectives Tauson and Neumann Interview Mike McLoren

Detective: Let me ask you about, uh . . . some marijuana that was in the drawer of your . . . fort? Tell us about that.

McLoren: It's like, I had it to smoke it.

Detective: Okay. How much was there?

McLoren: Uh . . . maybe like a half-ounce.

Detective: Did you have it, uh . . . separated into . . . Baggies?

McLoren: I think it was.

Detective: Have you ever sold marijuana?

McLoren: Nah.

•

When asked what they'd been doing before the fight ensued, Mike explained that he and Jimmy had come home from school that afternoon to hang out in the fort with Mike's girlfriend, Stacey Williams, and her friend, Natasha Sinkinson. Classmates John Berardis and Johnny Vinnedge also showed up. The six friends watched the movie *Pulp Fiction* on video. The film had been released in theaters only seven months before, and although back in 1995 viewers had to wait at least a year or two before watching major releases on their home videocassette recorders, one of the friends had taken the video from another friend's dad in the film industry. At some point in the late afternoon, Chris Velardo, Natasha's boyfriend, also stopped by for a bit. He didn't stay long.

Mike explained that later, after Stacey, Natasha, John, and Johnny had left, he ran up to the house to eat a quick dinner with his mother and grandparents, while Jimmy waited inside the fort. When Mike returned after about fifteen minutes, he and Jimmy stood outside the fort pounding the giant punching bag. They saw four boys they knew climb over his chain-link fence, then walk "boldly" toward the fort.

McLoren: They . . . they came up to me and they said, "Gimme the keys, fool." I can't remember if I said like, "What keys?" or "You don't get any keys."

Detective: Who said, "Where's the keys?"

McLoren: Micah.

Detective: Micah?

McLoren: Yeah. And like, I told him he couldn't have 'em. And then he was like, "What! You startin' shit with the Gumbys, *ese*?"

(PAUSE)

McLoren: 'Cause like, Jim comes in, and he starts sockin' 'em. And it's like, I'm tryin' to elbow 'em in the head, and I kicked 'em in the face. Hmm . . . I seem to have had Micah under me. And I see his head right here, so I start elbowing it with the back of my elbow right in his neck. Yeah, and I remember I had Micah, and I was elbowing him in the head. And his brother came up and tried to grab me, and I kicked him in the face, I think.

When the detectives specifically asked where exactly Chris Velardo was, Mike responded that he'd never actually seen Chris's face. Mike changed his story a number of times during the interview. As he was recounting the events, then modifying them, then replaying them again, Detective Neumann interrupted Mike and said, "Do you know a Tony Miliotti?"

"Yeah!" Mike answered. "He might have been there. Actually, I think he was one of the ones in there! And maybe Chris Velardo drove there? I don't know. That's like, that seems like it rings something in my head, though."

Detective: Where was Jimmy?

McLoren: Like, Jimmy is bent over, and like, the Brandon guy is like . . . um . . . like socking him with uppercuts or something like that. Umm . . . it's like . . . I think the guy who stabbed Jimmy, though, was, like, Brandon . . .

Detective: Did you see him stab him?

McLoren: Maybe that's what I saw, and it wasn't a punch! I don't know.

Detective: Okay.

McLoren: 'Cause they like . . . YEAH they stabbed me. Yeah they all stabbed me. I remember they traded the knife, I think.

Detective: Did you see who was holding the knife?

McLoren: I think it was Micah's knife. I think they actually took turns like, like getting their shots in, you know?

Detective: Well, what did you see?

McLoren: I didn't, like, really SEE anything.

Detective: Has your memory improved since you've . . .

McLoren: Yeah.

Detective: Uh . . . as the days go by?

McLoren: Yeah.

Detective: Okay, maybe we'll . . . uh, later come back and
talk to you, too. We want you to think about it.

Before the officers left the hospital, Detective Neumann asked Mike one last question. "So, in your opinion, what was this all about? Why did these guys come over to your place?"

Mike McLoren shrugged. "I think they were seriously just bored. So they just say, 'I know where we can get a free TV, VCR, you know, all that stuff.' Because I had it all in my fort, you know. And it's like, 'How easy would it be to get all new free stuff? And maybe, even, like a little bit of marijuana to go with it,' you know." Mike was speculating at the time. He had no proof that these were the people who had stolen from him before this. And he had no proof that was the reason for their visit on Monday. Still, this story stuck, and it later served as the prosecution's only "proof" of an attempted robbery.

Detectives Tauson and Neumann then told Mike they would visit him at his home in a few days, after his release from the hospital. They wished him well and let him know they were in a bit of a rush. The officers were on their way to pay respects to Mike's longtime best friend, Jimmy Farris. His funeral was set to begin.

THE FUNERAL

IT'S SAFE TO ASSUME THAT THERE IS NO PAIN MORE
severe than that suffered while burying a child, especially a
healthy, loving child in the prime of his life. Jim Farris Senior
summed it up best on the day of the funeral when he said, "It's a
senseless, out-of-sequence, and stupid thing."

More than three hundred fifty mourners gathered in the cool,
damp morning of Friday, May 26, on the rolling lawns of the Pierce
Brothers Valley Oaks Mortuary in Westlake Village, just two miles
from the Farris home. The crowd included Agoura High School students and several Los Angeles Police Department officers. Though
the Farris family kept the service private, and the press was not
invited to attend, newspaper reporters and television cameras
gathered outside the giant ring of flags surrounding the ceremony.

Afterward, Jim Farris Senior and Jimmy's twenty-three-year-
old brother, Travis, spoke to reporters, their swollen eyes hidden

behind sunglasses. Travis appeared to be a more mature twin of his little brother Jimmy, with his same eyes, hair, and demeanor. Jim Farris Senior rivaled tough-guy Old West cowboys with his rugged good looks and confident swagger. "I've been crying for days," Travis told them. He, understandably, found it difficult to rein in his anger. "Those . . . monsters who killed him didn't know Jimmy. He stepped in and did what he always did." His family described a "family-oriented" kid, who loved to hunt and fish with his father and ride motorcycles. "Protective" was the word used most often to describe Jimmy.

Judie Farris couldn't bring herself to speak to reporters. A striking blond beauty, Judie shared Jimmy's outgoing nature. She was personable, but tough. Never one to hold her tongue or hide her emotions, Judie Farris was the kind of enigmatic mom who seemed like she could wrestle a steer at the rodeo just as easily as she could grace the covers of women's high-fashion magazines.

Friends and classmates agreed that Jimmy was the epitome of the all-American boy. They labeled him "outgoing," "energetic," and "genuine." His good friend Eldar Adi remembered Jimmy teaching him to ride a motorcycle at the young age of ten. Jimmy loved the USA, often shouted it from the rooftops, and dreamed of becoming a police officer or joining the military. Eldar said he and other friends visited Mike McLoren's fort on many occasions to watch movies and play video games with Mike and Jimmy. He recalled happy memories. Still, his opinion was that the fort really needed to be torn down. He said Mike's grandparents never liked it, and it "just brought trouble."

CHARGES

AT THE JUVENILE ARRAIGNMENT IN SYLMAR JUVENILE
Court on Tuesday, May 30, both Micah and Chris pleaded not
guilty to charges of robbery, attempted murder, and murder.
Attorney Bruce Jones spoke for his client, Chris Velardo. He
began by saying, "I have a very sweet, very clean client, who is
being kept in custody with a bunch of hard cases."

Indeed, the Barry J. Nidorf facility in Sylmar was closer to
an adult prison than an actual juvenile jail. Boys imprisoned
in this facility were those who had lost their "fitness" trials. In
other words, they were deemed unfit to be tried as juveniles and
were awaiting their trials in adult court, which would later produce adult sentences. Most of their cases involved gang-related
charges of murder and attempted murder. Though these boys
were all between the ages of twelve and seventeen, their childhoods were over.

By law these youths were required to receive at least an hour of recreation per day, several hours of schooling on the weekdays, and access to programming designed for rehabilitation. In reality, many were placed in solitary confinement for days or weeks at a time, some were on suicide watch—which required that a staff member remain within touching distance at all times—and others were so heavily medicated with sedatives that they did nothing but sleep and occasionally eat. These prisoners were lucky to enjoy an hour or two per week of "recreation," which usually involved standing outside the compound walls in tiny fenced-in cages, with nothing to do but walk in circles. Donated basketballs, now flat, littered the yard. Slivers of plastic Frisbee remnants lingered here and there. Occasionally, one was fortunate enough to find a rubber handball or tennis ball lying around that could be tossed back and forth. Because the wait for an adult trial could often take a few years, many inmates had been there long enough to create and enforce gang rules and a sophisticated hierarchy system. The politics at the Sylmar facility rivaled those of hard-core maximum-security prisons. There was nothing juvenile about this place.

Bruce Jones continued presenting his case in favor of setting his client free. He urged the judge to consider the fact that Chris Velardo had never even left his truck while the other boys entered the property. Mike McLoren had clearly been confused and mistaken when he'd said Chris had been present during the fight, maybe because he had seen Chris a few hours earlier. Not only that, but Chris also had no idea that anybody had been stabbed.

There was no blood anywhere, and none of the other four boys said anything about a knife. Chris was told there'd been a brief fight, but he had never heard the whole story. Further, Bruce Jones explained that he could present "four people" who were told by Tony Miliotti that *he* had been involved in the fight and the stabbing, but Chris had not. According to Mr. Jones, Tony had informed these witnesses that it was he himself who held Jimmy Farris in a headlock, while Jason Holland stabbed him in the chest. Also according to Bruce Jones, Tony had told witnesses he was planning to turn himself in. Though Tony was not labeled a suspect, he was wanted for questioning. But when authorities went to his home to inquire about the fight, they said, "he had vanished." This information didn't look good for Tony. And Bruce Jones hoped it could help exonerate his client.

Micah's attorney, John Franklin, added another previously unknown piece to the puzzle. This event was never a robbery. It wasn't even an attempted robbery. It was simply a marijuana deal gone bad. The boys had driven over to McLoren's house earlier in the day to purchase marijuana and were told to come back later when he would have an additional stash. When they returned, Mike and Micah exchanged words, and that led to a fight.

The judge decided to hold Chris and Micah in the Sylmar jail for a bit longer. He scheduled another hearing for June 16, where he would decide if there was enough evidence to order a trial for Chris or Micah. Chris had never even left the front seat of his truck. Micah had been beaten up by Mike McLoren, a teen who was one foot taller, two years older, and three dozen pounds heavier. According to everybody involved, neither Micah nor Chris had taken a single swing during the fight. Was there enough evidence to warrant a murder trial for these two kids who had never hurt anybody? Unfortunately, the boys would now have to wait another two weeks to find out.

HEARING

ALTHOUGH TONY WAS ORIGINALLY WANTED ONLY for questioning, on Thursday, June 1, homicide detectives issued a warrant for his arrest. Just after six p.m. on Friday, June 2, Tony turned himself in to the Lost Hills Sheriff's Station. He was accompanied by his family. He had a huge local extended family of aunts, uncles, and cousins, who were all extremely close. Like the other boys, he was immediately charged with robbery, attempted murder, and murder. Tony also denied the charges just before he was transported from the Lost Hills Sheriff's Station holding cell to the Sylmar jail on Wednesday, June 7.

That same day, a preliminary hearing was held to determine Brandon Hein's fate. Was there enough evidence to hold Brandon and force him to stand trial for murder? One judge, James Albracht, would decide. Since he was already eighteen years old, Brandon had been housed in the Los Angeles County Men's

Central Jail. Placed in a modified unit, he was able to remain in a single cell for the duration of the proceedings. His attorney, Jill Lansing, had been granted this arrangement for protective purposes because the case was becoming so high profile. When murder cases turn into big news, a defendant's safety is always at risk. And because these charges involved a Los Angeles Police Department officer's son, Brandon's life was in especially grave danger.

Both detectives Neumann and Tauson put the story together as best they could while testifying during the hearing. Tauson described a violent brawl, evidenced by an upside-down plastic lawn chair and a "bloodied baseball bat." He said that he and Detective Neumann had interviewed Mike McLoren at his home during his recovery. At that time, Mike reported that four boys—Micah, Tony, Brandon, and Jason—had vaulted over his fence and approached him and Jimmy at the fort while they were exercising. They were "unsmiling," he said. Micah entered the fort first, pulling on the locked desk drawer and demanding the keys.

Incidentally, this was not the original story Mike had told officers, either right after the incident or when interviewed in the hospital. Mike said he followed Micah inside. Then Jason and Brandon entered the fort, then Jimmy. After Mike twice refused to hand over the keys, he said that "fists started flying and I got socked in the head like ten times." Also during this hearing, Neumann related Mike's story that Jason, Micah, and Brandon had all three punched him at the same time. Although Mike had previously told detectives he "didn't actually *see* anything," while engaged in the fight, during the home interview he claimed he saw Jason and Micah, the Holland brothers, pass the knife back and forth. Mike said he also saw Jimmy sitting on a mattress while being punched in the face repeatedly by Brandon Hein. Jimmy never fought back. Mike said he was then kicked into a corner of the fort and found an opportunity for escape. That was when he and Jimmy ran to the main house.

After the detectives gave their testimony, Brandon Hein's attorney, Jill Lansing, reminded Judge James Albracht that since nothing was missing from the fort, nor were any of the defendants' fingerprints found on the locked desk drawer or anywhere else, there was no evidence of a robbery, or even an attempted robbery. Further, she did not believe Brandon should legally face a murder trial, since there was also no evidence that he had stabbed anybody or even touched anybody.

While the Hein family waited for the judge's decision, Sharry Holland was turning to TV cameras outside the Malibu Municipal Courthouse. She expressed her love for Jason and begged him to turn himself in. She reiterated to reporters that she had heard nothing from him since the night of Monday, May 22. Her last contact with Jason was when he said "I love you" three times through the phone, then hung up. Two mothers prayed for the lives of their eighteen-year-old sons, which up until two weeks ago had been relatively trouble free.

At the end of the day, Gene and Pat Hein (Brandon's biological mother) watched their young son—his small body trembling, his head hanging low—sit at the front of the courtroom, dressed in his oversize orange jumpsuit with LA COUNTY JAIL emblazoned on the back, waiting to hear one judge make a colossal ruling that could change the trajectories of their lives.

Finally Judge Albracht asked Brandon to stand. He stared straight down at the boy, who stood less than five and one half feet tall. The judge stated that, yes, Brandon Hein had in fact "aided and abetted" in the attempted robbery and stabbing of Jimmy Farris and Mike McLoren. Brandon would, therefore, be ordered to stand trial for robbery, attempted murder, and murder. He would be held without bail. Brandon's mother, Pat, exploded into sobs.

SURRENDER

SHARRY HOLLAND HAD SPENT THREE PAINFUL WEEKS hoping to hear something—anything—from her son Jason. No family members had heard from him. None of his friends knew his whereabouts. *America's Most Wanted*, the Fox Television Network's hit show profiling cases of fugitives wanted for committing the most heinous crimes like murder, rape, kidnapping, and acts of terrorism, had aired a special episode seeking information about Jason's location. Viewers were instructed to call the tip line at 1-800-Holland with any pertinent information, and a mug shot of Jason from two years before was repeatedly broadcast on the national show. In his eighteen years, Jason had had only one minor scuffle with the law, when he was apprehended at age sixteen for spray-painting graffiti on a freeway overpass. Police now reported that they had every agency imaginable searching for him. One FBI officer said Jason had been spotted out in the Palm Springs desert, his hair dyed jet-black.

During those three long weeks, Sharry grew depressed, anxious, and unable to concentrate on her work in real estate sales. She had lost both of her sons in one night and had difficulty caring for her young daughter, Kylie. "I don't even know how to tell her," Sharry confessed to reporters. "How do you explain this to a five-year-old?" She sent Kylie to live with relatives for a while.

Just after one a.m. on the morning of Sunday, June 11, Sharry Holland was once again rattled by the sound of knocking on the front door at her Thousand Oaks apartment. Jason stood on the front step, unkempt and fatigued. Mother and son embraced, then cried and hugged for a while, she said. Fully understanding that that this was possibly the last time she and her son would share a moment of time alone, Sharry refused to question Jason about the night Jimmy was killed. She tried to cook food for him, but he couldn't eat. So they took deep breaths and prepared to do the honorable thing right then and there. Jason brushed his teeth and pulled on a fresh pair of shoes.

Within the hour a family friend came over and drove the two to the Lost Hills Sheriff's Station. Jason and Sharry held hands in the backseat for the short ride. They didn't speak. Later, Sharry described Jason as seeming sad, but not necessarily nervous. At the station, mother and son hugged one last time, then parted, and Jason was led down the hallway to the interrogation room. Before disappearing, he turned around to see his mother one last time.

"I love you," he said.

"I love you, too, babe."

NOT SO SPEEDY

THE SIXTH AMENDMENT TO THE UNITED STATES Constitution provides criminal defendants with seven personal liberties, the first of which is the right to a speedy trial. Rooted in twelfth-century England, the right to a speedy trial exists because it is unfair to force innocent humans to suffer in jail for lengthy periods of time before they have even been convicted of a crime. After all, every defendant is supposed to be innocent until proven guilty. Furthermore, as time drags on before the commencement of a trial, weeks and months have a way of making memories fade and witnesses and evidence vanish.

As anyone who has ever been arrested for a crime can attest, the US Constitution uses the word *speedy* loosely. Once someone is arrested, the police must complete a report that describes events leading up to the crime, identifies witnesses' names and claims, and lists any potential crimes that warranted the defendant being arrested. Once the defendant is in custody, the prosecutor has forty-eight hours to decide which charges will be filed. Weekends, holidays, and court closure days don't count as part of the forty-eight hours, so in reality it can take longer. Defendants then attend an arraignment, which is the first time they ever appear in court. At this time the judge tells the defendant what he is being charged with, lists his constitutional rights, and explains that a court-appointed lawyer shall be provided if he cannot afford one. The defendant pleads guilty, not guilty, or no contest, which basically means, *I know I'm screwed, but I don't confirm or deny committing the crime.*

A judge then does one of three things. He can release the defendant on his own recognizance, where the suspect promises not to flee. He can set bail, or an amount of money the defendant can pay to be released until future court dates. Or he can refuse to set bail, and send the defendant back to jail, where he will live for the remainder of the proceedings until the trial is over. In setting a bail amount, or refusing to set bail, a judge must consider whether the defendant is an immediate threat to the public, and whether he has family and connections in the community who can support him through the trial process. After this arraignment, the judge holds a preliminary hearing, where he listens to all the information and decides if there is enough valid evidence to suggest that the defendant committed the crime. If yes, then a trial is ordered for a later date. The prosecutor files a manuscript called the Information, which must be filed within fifteen days of the preliminary hearing. A second arraignment is set to discuss the Information. During this second arraignment, the defendant can change his plea. By California law, the trial must begin within sixty days of the second arraignment on the Information.

In the weeks and months before a trial, the defense attorneys and prosecutors must exchange all information about the case, which is called "discovery." Attorneys from both sides can talk among themselves or with the judge about how the case can be resolved with plea deals without ever going to trial. A defendant can change his plea at any time. Either side can also file pretrial motions, where they can ask to dismiss the case altogether or present reasons why certain evidence should be excluded from the trial.

The defendant can choose whether he would like to be tried by a jury of his peers, or have a court trial, where only a judge hears the evidence and decides his fate. The majority of the time, people prefer to have a trial by jury, because, quite honestly, who wants to place the fate of his entire life in the hands of one person who may be having a bad day? Once a trial date is set, and a jury that is acceptable to both the defense and the prosecution is chosen, the trial starts with opening statements. Witnesses are then called to the stand and asked questions by both sides. The trial concludes with closing arguments. In order for a jury to convict a defendant of a felony, he must be found guilty *beyond a reasonable doubt*. In other words, there can be no other reasonable explanation other than the defendant committed the crime. Blackstone's Formulation is the principle upon which our courts were formed. Sir William Blackstone said in 1760, "It is better that ten guilty persons escape, than that one innocent suffer." Therefore, an entire jury must be 100 percent certain of a person's guilt in order to convict him and send him to prison.

Friday, June 16, was the date that Micah, Chris—and now Tony—had been waiting for. Tony had been incarcerated in the Sylmar juvenile facility for only two weeks. Micah and Chris had been there nearly an entire month, waiting for the juvenile court commissioner to decide if there was enough evidence presented to necessitate a murder trial for the three boys. They woke up early that Friday with the giddy anticipation that they could actually be freed within the next twelve hours. No more concrete slabs for beds, mushy bread and moldy lunch meat for meals, or hours upon hours of isolation rotting inside ten-foot-by-ten-foot cells, where the temperatures fluctuated from damp and frosty to sweltering and muggy. Comfort of the inhabitants was apparently not a priority at the Sylmar jail. Or, more likely, discomfort of the inmates was the point.

But when the boys were led into the courtroom, they learned that Curtis Leftwich, Tony's recently appointed attorney, had just requested a continuance for the juvenile hearing, claiming that he had not had enough time to prepare for his client's case. In his defense, Leftwich was already juggling dozens of criminal cases, some of which were high-profile gang-related murders. Juvenile Court Commissioner Jack Gold agreed that, yes, in order for Mr. Leftwich to represent his client effectively, a postponement was necessary. The hearing to decide if the boys would actually face a trial would be moved to July 24, nearly two months after

Jimmy Farris's murder. If the boys were ordered to stand trial, an additional hearing would be held that day to determine whether they should be tried in juvenile or adult court. Once again, the fate of these boys hovered in the air like a hawk waiting to dive-bomb its prey. Micah, Chris, and Tony were learning the hard way how vague the term *speedy* really was.

Finally, on the morning of Monday, July 24, the three boys were led into the tiny courtroom next to the Sylmar jail. Clad in their oversize jumpsuits, the boys nodded to their family members, who had been waiting on eggshells. The mood was somber. The once healthy, bright-eyed boys now appeared pale and sickly, with clusters of acne developing on each of their faces. The three boys kept their heads down during the hearing, but they undoubtedly hung on every word, praying to hear something positive.

Prosecutor Jeffrey Semow, a small, handsome man with Ken-doll-perfect hair and what appeared to be a perpetual smirk, stood before the court and laid into the boys. What he lacked in stature, Semow made up for in his bark. The boys had driven to Mike McLoren's home for the sole purpose of robbing him of his marijuana, Semow said. And every single one of them knew that somebody had a knife, he insisted.

The defense attorneys tried to argue that since nothing had been taken from the fort, there was no robbery. Since nobody knew who had stabbed Jimmy and Mike, perhaps it was an accident.

The teens had just stolen a woman's wallet from a park on the way over there, Semow shot back, implying that they were "on a crime spree" and knew exactly what they were doing.

Chris Velardo's attorney, Bruce Jones, argued that Chris knew nothing of a robbery and was the "equivalent of a taxicab driver."

"It's highly improbable that the other four acted as they did with a common plan, and left Velardo out of that plan," Semow said. He also suggested that the plan was highly sophisticated, and Micah—although the youngest and the smallest—was the ringleader.

John Franklin, attorney for Micah, said the plan was "anything but sophisticated," and added that "nobody was more surprised than these kids here" that Jimmy was actually stabbed with a knife.

For four full days this went on, each side repeating theories and guesses and shouting at the other side. Attorney John Franklin often attacked Mike McLoren's credibility. After all, he had initially reported that the boys demanded that he hand over his television and VCR, and they all had knives. Later, he claimed that they had demanded marijuana, and he never actually saw a knife at all. He never could remember who threw the first punch.

Toward the end of the day on Thursday, July 27, Commissioner Jack Gold looked at the three boys, then looked to their families and said, "They all got together and were out for no good." Micah, Chris, and Tony sat emotionless. After agreeing that the crimes were indeed "sophisticated," Commissioner Gold reminded the boys that if their cases stayed in the juvenile system, they could potentially be locked up until their twenty-fifth birthdays. That meant serving eight to ten years of hard-core prison time. A harsh sentence, especially for one barely pubescent boy who had been severely beaten by McLoren, one boy who stood in a doorway watching a fight, and one who'd never even left the front seat of his truck across the street. Shockingly, that was the best-case scenario. On the other hand, moving their trials to adult court could mean life sentences for all.

Finally Commissioner Gold declared that Micah, Chris, and Tony would all stand trial as adults. Arraignment on charges of murder and attempted murder was scheduled for Thursday, August 17, in the Malibu Municipal Courthouse, where Brandon and Jason would also stand trial. All five boys now officially faced murder raps and life in prison.

BAD NEWS AND WORSE NEWS

THREE MORE WEEKS PASSED BEFORE ANY OF THE FIVE boys received word on where their cases were headed. Jason and Brandon stayed in the Los Angeles County Men's Central Jail, held without bail. Micah and Tony remained incarcerated in the Sylmar jail, held without bail. And Chris, who by all accounts had simply sat in his pickup truck while the attack occurred, was housed in Sylmar as well, held on one million dollars bail.

On Friday, August 18, Micah, Chris, Tony, Brandon, and Jason faced Superior Court Judge Lawrence Mira and awaited his decision on when their trials would begin. An intimidating figure, Judge Mira looked like a stereotypical judge from a cartoon. White hair topped his full, leathery face. Stern eyes and fluffy gray eyebrows sat behind round glasses. His expression seemed frozen in a permanent scowl.

A few dozen friends and family members crowded into the

cramped courtroom in Malibu. All five boys undoubtedly snuck glances at the giant oil painting hanging on the wall. How could they not? Beautifully ominous, it featured the watery splendor of Alcatraz prison. A twenty-two-acre rocky island one mile off the San Francisco shore, Alcatraz was the most infamous federal prison in the world from 1934 to 1963. Designed to house bank robbers and murderers who constantly caused trouble in other US penitentiaries, Alcatraz Island was home to the most notorious and violent mobsters and criminals in American history.

Prosecutor Jeffrey Semow reminded the judge that although Mike McLoren never actually saw who stabbed him or Jimmy, all five boys should be held criminally responsible for the murder. Judge Mira then made a shocking announcement. "This was a single incident with allegedly five participants. So it seems to me this must be consolidated." This meant the five boys would be tried all together. The trial was set for October 6, 1995, more than four months after the incident. Consolidation of defendants' cases into one trial was a bold move on the part of the prosecution and a huge drawback for the defense. The five boys most likely all had different levels of culpability in Jimmy Farris's death. And lumping them together suggested they were all equally responsible. It would be difficult for a jury to separate them and their actions. These types of trials are generally nightmares for defense attorneys and their defendants, because sometimes an attorney feels like he or she must toss another defendant under the bus in order to make his client look better. This ruling spelled disaster.

Before the day was over, Prosecutor Semow also made a startling announcement. Because Jason and Brandon were legal adults at the time of the attack, their charges were labeled as "murder with special circumstances." In California, not all murders are created equal. In order for a murder to be the worst possible type, it must have a "special circumstance" attached. These circumstances have changed over the years, but generally include murder during a bombing, murder of a police officer or judge, or murder during the course of a felony. California felonies include rape, kidnapping, arson, carjacking, and robbery. The special circumstance in this case was a murder during the commission of a felony. The felony? The robbery of Mike McLoren's marijuana. Though no robbery took place, the prosecutor said that the intent to rob was enough to tag the boys with a felony. The worst part about this "special circumstance" label? It potentially carried the worst possible sentence for Jason and Brandon—

The death penalty.

LIFE OR DEATH?

SINCE THE CALIFORNIA DEATH PENALTY WAS restored in 1977, more than nine hundred prisoners have received the death sentence. But up until 1992, the state had not executed anybody in twenty-five years. Now the death penalty was making a comeback.

Forty-eight-year-old William George Bonin was scheduled for execution by the State of California on February 23, 1996, six months from the day that eighteen-year-olds Jason and Brandon learned they would potentially face the same fate. Bonin was to become the first inmate in California to be killed by lethal injection, rather than the gas chamber. He had his choice between the two.

Described by Prosecutor Aaron Stovitz as "the most arch-evil person who ever existed," William Bonin, labeled the Freeway Killer, was born in Connecticut and had earned Good Conduct medals during his brief service in the Vietnam War when he was quite young. Sixteen years before his date with death, he had been arrested for abducting, torturing, and killing at least twenty-one boys in Southern California. Though he had twenty-one proven victims at the time of his trial, it is more than likely that he had killed another fifteen for which he was never charged. Bonin's modus operandi was to lure older teen boys who were hitch-hiking, waiting for buses, biking, or walking alone into his van. Then he raped, tortured, and mutilated them before strangling them with their own shirts. Several were also stabbed with ice picks. He dumped every one of their bodies right on the sides of the California freeways. His spree lasted only ten months, from August 1979 through June 1980. But the psychopathic bender was arguably one of the most heinous in American history in terms of brutality, as far as serial killers go.

This was the type of man with whom Jason and Brandon could now look forward to sharing cell space. Regardless of one's position on the death penalty, this barbaric sentence was undoubt-edly invented for the purpose of eliminating the worst of the worst humans, those who cannot be rehabilitated. Someone like a William George Bonin. Someone who spent most of his waking hours of an entire year kidnapping, raping, mutilating, then kill-ing thirty-six teen boys. Ironically, all his victims were roughly the same age as Jason and Brandon. One would be hard-pressed to find anyone with half a brain who could place Jason Holland and Brandon Hein in the same category as a serial kidnapper, rapist, and child killer.

Fortunately for Jason and Brandon, on Wednesday, September

13, Assistant Head Deputy District Attorney Lael Rubin announced that her office had decided to dismiss the death penalty as a possible sentence. She further said that, "age was certainly a factor" and that the harsh sentence seemed inappropriate for the teen defendants.

Relief.

For the time being.

SECRETS

ON FRIDAY, SEPTEMBER 15, UNEXPECTED THINGS began brewing. Apparently, for several weeks Judge Mira had been pressuring prosecutor Jeffrey Semow to hand over some special secret evidence that he had been withholding from the defense team. Semow had been consistently refusing to give it up, claiming it would clash with his "ethics." Too bad, Judge Mira ruled. He gave Semow one last chance to turn over these secret documents. In fact, he had mere minutes to do so. If he did not, Judge Mira promised to slam his wooden gavel, dismiss all charges, and let all five defendants go home.

Within seconds of this demand, Semow distributed the super-secret documents to all five defense attorneys. After reading the pages, Tony Miliotti's attorney, Curtis Leftwich, requested immediate protection for his client. Velardo's new attorney, Charles English, then requested the same for Chris. Without hesitating,

Judge Mira agreed to keep both Tony and Chris in the Sylmar juvenile facility, and move Micah somewhere else. He guaranteed them that Chris and Tony would have no contact with the other three defendants. All attorneys requested that the documents be kept private, so they were unavailable to the press or public. The contents were never revealed in open court.

Micah had seen and talked briefly with both Chris Velardo and Tony Miliotti back in Sylmar. Although they were separated, they'd occasionally pass one another on their way to recreation or chapel. Through these conversations, Micah surmised that the prosecution team was trying to get Chris and Tony to flip. In other words, because Chris and Tony were being labeled as the least culpable in Jimmy Farris's death, Jeffrey Semow and the police were most likely pressuring the two boys to snitch on their friends in exchange for deals. The prosecution needed to tag a robbery charge on these guys. And in order to do that, they needed Tony or Chris to testify that they had all driven to Mike McLoren's house on that Monday afternoon with the intention of stealing something. That testimony would strengthen Mike McLoren's story that there was an attempted robbery.

Tony assured Micah that he'd never take a deal, and never snitch or lie or do anything to harm his friends. Even if they offered Tony an agreement where he could avoid a trial by telling them what they wanted to hear, he'd say no. Micah's guess was that this supersecret information the prosecution was now handing out probably had something to do with these deals being offered and the pressuring of Chris and Tony. Micah was young. But he was smart. He could size up anybody in just a few seconds, and he could certainly smell manipulation. Still, if Tony did take a deal, Micah told him, he totally understood and would never hold it against him. They were all in survival mode now. Dog eat dog. Every man for himself. Look out for number one, and all that.

Micah was promptly moved to Central Juvenile Hall on Eastlake Avenue in downtown Los Angeles. Central was a gloomy facility resembling most other jails and prisons in California. It had the requisite high walls topped with razor wire, giant metal rolling fences that opened to squad cars and transport vans, and a series of electronic gates leading to the reception area. Security was beyond tight.

Each building held two units, and they were broken up into letters A/B, C/D, and so on. Central Juvenile Hall, or CJH, housed roughly six hundred inmates, all awaiting trials. The units were broken up primarily according to gender, age, and crime. Some inmates were as young as twelve years old. Only a few units housed girls. The vast majority of juvenile offenders were male. Girls' units and boys' units never interacted. The only time inmates could see somebody of the opposite sex was if they happened to have a cell with a window facing toward the chapel or the Al Jones Store—the canteen, where each unit was led single file to purchase snacks once a week.

Micah was given his new wardrobe, a gray T-shirt and loose black pants resembling a doctor's scrubs. He was cuffed, shackled, then led across the yard, which was really a giant flat football-field-size plot of dirt and grass. He could see a basketball court toward the far end of the facility, a blacktop with two hoops but no nets. Scrawny feral cats lurked everywhere, scuttling from building to building, then disappearing into the corners. The officer leading Micah stopped him at the K/L building. All units looked exactly the same, dirty brick walls dotted with tiny scratched-up foggy windows. But Micah knew that K/L weren't like the other units at CJH. These were reserved for only the high-risk offenders, or kids who were facing trials as adults for alleged crimes of murder, attempted murder, and the like. Housing primarily hard-core gang members, the K/L units were affectionately called "the Killer Units."

He was welcomed to his new home by Officer Sills, an enormous guard with a barrel chest and the frame of a pro football player. A man of few words, but poignant advice, according to Micah he said, "You're the smallest kid here. You're also the whitest kid here. You'd better learn to fight."

Micah did. Quickly. He also learned how to score drugs. Lots of drugs. Years later, Micah said, "Everyone was high all the time in Central." Sometimes staff members inadvertently operated as drug mules. At the time, CJH had pretty relaxed rules about perks for the inmates. After all, they were still children, weren't they? During school hours, kids could have home-cooked meals delivered from their families. One popular teacher—who happened to be a former LAPD cop—even did rounds, driving to homes to pick up the food, then delivering it to the classroom. Micah was surprised to learn that many of the students were using the food to have their drugs delivered, without their teacher ever knowing. Moms, dads, and siblings were stuffing Baggies of heroin and pills into burritos! Back then, nearly anything could also easily be smuggled into Central Juvenile Hall during inmate visits with family members. That perk of bringing in gifts was discontinued when one mother baked a birthday cake and brought it to her son during visiting hours. Upon scanning it through the metal detector at the entrance, guards noticed it had a gun inside.

Once he hit puberty, Micah also learned from his fellow inmates how to "bust a Fifi." Since inmates could not have any contact with members of the opposite sex, they became creative. Fifi referred to a simulated vagina, fashioned from a CJH hand towel twisted up and looped into a circle with a hole in the middle. Inmates added liquid soap, and voilà! Instant sex. This trick would come in handy, especially for those who lost their fitness trials and were heading to serve long sentences well into adulthood.

PLEA DEAL

ON THURSDAY, SEPTEMBER 28, CHRIS VELARDO
turned eighteen. He also had an announcement. He had a change
of heart. Chris traded his not guilty plea. Instead he pled guilty
to one count of conspiracy to commit robbery. Then he pled
guilty to voluntary manslaughter. In general, manslaughter is
described as the least negative definition of murder. Often called
a "heat of the moment" killing, voluntary manslaughter is a murder that was not premeditated, but was the result of provocation.
Again, Chris never left his truck, did not touch either of the victims, nor did he even witness the fight.

Taking a plea deal is very common, and it does not mean that
the defendant is actually admitting guilt. It's simply a way to
avoid a lengthy trial where a life is in the hands of a jury. And
juries are notoriously unpredictable. There's an old saying that
the only sure things in life are death and taxes, but you can also

call it a fact that nobody on the planet can predict a jury verdict with certainty. Chris was scheduled for sentencing on November 28, exactly one month away, and was told he was facing a maximum sentence of twelve years.

The conundrum for someone like Chris Velardo was pretty straightforward, yet dicey. He could maintain his not guilty plea and toss the dice with the other four boys in hopes that a jury would find them innocent and set them free. On the other hand, the worst-case scenario meant that the jury could find him guilty and he'd spend the rest of his life in prison. Actually, all of them were facing not just life in prison, but LWOPP—life without the possibility of parole. Usually, not even an act of God can wiggle you out of an LWOPP sentence. Those sentences are rarely commuted or won on appeal. Or Chris could take the deal offered to him by the prosecutors, plead guilty (even if he wasn't guilty of anything), knowing he would be handed a finite sentence that would be over in twelve years at the most. In that case, he would be released before the age of thirty and could still have a chance at some kind of life.

This is the ultimate gamble for someone involved—even peripherally—in a heinous crime where they are facing a life sentence. It is also the type of deal that thousands of Americans face every year once they are thrown into the criminal justice system. In this case, it seemed unlikely that any jury would find Chris guilty of murder. However, now that their trials were consolidated into one, he couldn't be so sure.

Still, would a jury actually find all five boys guilty of first-degree murder, when Jimmy Farris's death was most likely an accident and an unintended consequence of a common fistfight? Chris's attorney, Charles English, was smart. This wasn't his first rodeo, and he had undoubtedly seen too many of the "worst-case scenarios" at the conclusions of jury trials. He was most likely very familiar with Jeffrey Semow's prosecution skills. As large as Los Angeles is, the world of criminal defense and prosecution is amazingly small. English probably knew the prosecution was crafty and cooking up something.

"This is in no way a deal for testimony," Semow said. This meant that although Chris seemed to be "turning" on his friends, that wasn't actually the case. Many times defendants are offered plea deals as favors from the prosecution. In exchange, they have to snitch on their codefendants, or tell the prosecution what they want to hear. But Semow said he might never call Chris to testify on the stand, and even if he did, Chris could cite his Fifth Amendment rights. When someone "takes the Fifth," they are refusing to answer questions that could incriminate them.

It's interesting that one of the last things prosecutor Semow said at the hearing was, "Mr. Velardo remained in the truck while all the other defendants went over the fence and into the fort. There is no evidence that he knew or intended that anybody would be injured." So Semow was making it sound like they were cutting Chris Velardo a break since he was nowhere near the fight. Still, the prosecutors were charging Chris with homicide because they were convinced that the whole thing was intended to be a robbery. How could someone nowhere near a slaying end up charged with murder?

FELONY MURDER RULE

AN ANTIQUATED LAW WITH ITS ROOTS IN 1500S England, the felony murder rule states that if somebody is in the process of committing a felony (rape, kidnapping, carjacking, bombing, robbery) and a person accidentally dies, anyone who participated—even loosely—is fully responsible for that murder in the first degree. One can literally be found guilty by association. There needn't be any intent to kill or maim, and every participant is equally responsible and will probably face the same sentence, even if they had no knowledge of the impending killing. The rule is often applied to people who drive getaway cars, even if they were not present during the crime. The contemporary warning is supposed to be: choose your friends wisely.

In general, scholars believe the law was intended to punish those groups of people who ran into banks or trains and shot up the places while robbing them. Before forensic evidence became technologically advanced, it was difficult to discern who shot the exact bullet that caused a death in these situations. Therefore, all participants were treated the same. Most developed countries have abolished the felony murder rule because it leads to cruel and unusual punishments. England, where the rule originated, took it off the books way back in 1957.

In its strictest form, felony murder can even apply to a death that accidentally occurs while preparing to commit a felony, or even during the flight afterward. In the early-morning hours of July 6, 2006, Cole Allen Wilkins of Long Beach, California, was driving down the 91 freeway with a bunch of appliances tied down to the back of his truck. One item, a large stove, slid underneath the ropes and tumbled into the middle of the freeway. Several cars stopped after hitting the stove. Another man was driving to work at five a.m. and swerved his car to avoid hitting the others. His car collided with a cement truck and he was crushed, killing him instantly. Cole Allen Wilkins was convicted of felony murder and sentenced to twenty-five years to life. Why? Wilkins had stolen the items in his truck, including the stove.

One of the most egregious misuses of the felony murder rule in recent history involved twenty-year-old Florida boy Ryan Holle in 2003. On the morning of March 10, Holle loaned his car to his roommate William Allen, something he had done on many occasions. William took three of his friends over to Christine Snyder's house with the intention of robbing her of a safe containing drugs and money. When they arrived, they found Snyder's teen daughter, Jessica, sleeping. One of the men,

Charles Miller, beat her to death with a shotgun he had found in the house. Afterward, they all returned to Ryan Holle's house with the safe, which contained a small amount of marijuana and a few hundred dollars.

The four men who drove to the Snyder home were all convicted of felony murder, because they had planned a burglary, even though none of the other three knew Miller would kill anybody, and he confessed. They were given sentences of life without parole. Ryan Holle was asleep at his home a mile away during the burglary and killing and had no knowledge of what the others were up to. He was also convicted of felony murder and given a sentence of life in prison without parole. The prosecutor held him just as responsible, and famously said, "No car, no murder." Ryan Holle said, "Of course I let them use my car. I honestly thought they were going out to get food!"

DELAYS

OCTOBER 6, 1995, THE DAY THE TRIAL WAS TO BEGIN, started with uncertainty. Again. Attorneys for both Jason and Micah Holland claimed that they were unprepared for the trial because new evidence had derailed them. They both asked for a sixty-day continuance.

Judge Mira agreed that there had in fact been many complications since he had set the trial date back in August, including the secret documents given to the defense by Jeffrey Semow two weeks earlier. "There is good cause to continue this case," he said.

Jill Lansing, Brandon Hein's attorney, vehemently disagreed and reminded the judge that this would infringe on his right to a speedy trial. Still, Judge Mira agreed that the trial needed to be delayed further. Whatever was in the secret documents seemed to be causing a lot of strife. And Judge Mira planned to keep the information concealed. An attorney for the *Los Angeles Times* filed a motion to release the transcripts of the private hearings that were allegedly detailed in the secret papers, but Mira denied the request. His concern, he said, was that once this information made its way into the public's knowledge, it could never "be forgotten," and it would be impossible to choose an impartial jury.

Judge Mira suggested a December trial date. It was quickly shot down by everybody, because it would conflict with their holiday vacations. It seemed the adults were forgetting that the lives of four teenage boys now hung in the balance. Delays are incredibly difficult and stressful for the accused. More importantly, everyone was forgetting that the incarcerated don't get holidays. Still, a January 8, 1996, date was set, more than seven months after the date of the event.

Nothing is ever easy in criminal trials. Nor are they ever truly speedy.

BACKGROUND

BY MID-OCTOBER 1995, THERE WAS STILL NO PUBLIC story about what actually took place that night in Mike McLoren's fort, either from the defendants, their families, or Mike himself. And nobody knew who had killed Jimmy Farris. Still, one thing was clear—this murder, this case, this upcoming trial was becoming a media circus, and talking about it or being the slightest bit connected to it became fashionable among the valley youth.

Funeral attendees paying their respects to Jimmy Farris back in May had marveled at how many kids had shown up, girls all dressed to impress. John Berardis, who was friends with both crews of boys, and who had partied in Mike's fort just hours before the murder, described the funeral services to *Rolling Stone* reporter Randall Sullivan. "There was, like, a thousand people acting like they were his friends . . . all the kids telling the cameras, 'Jimmy was the best.' Yeah, right. None of them gave a shit about that guy before. Jimmy never even had, like, a girlfriend. But all of a sudden, the day he dies, there are fifty girls saying they loved him." Berardis was clearly annoyed with not only the trendiness of the case, but the fact that a lot of the information presented in the press was just dead wrong. These types of events tend to shatter a community's way of thinking. Unfortunately, the more salacious a story, the more it sells. Back in 1995, there was no Internet. Or at least, it was still in its infancy. It was merely a spooky idea that sounded like science fiction to most. People actually had to pay good money to purchase hard copies of newspapers and magazines. Scandal sells. The more drama, the better.

On October 22, 1995, the *Los Angeles Times* ran an article written by Mary Pols that summed up the case to that point. Mary was also awed by the festive nature of the recent court hearings. She described a pack of pretty young girls primping in the Malibu Courthouse parking lot, laughing, smoking, and struggling to walk on heels that were way too high, then pushing their way into the courthouse all the way up to the front row to snatch good seats, as if they were attending a concert. They giggled, waved, and whispered as the defendants were led into the room wearing their brightly colored Los Angeles County jail jumpsuits.

The former girlfriend of one of the defendants expressed her frustration at how her peers treated the case and the court hearings like entertainment. "It's the cool thing to do. It's a trend right now. These girls are young and dumb and don't know what they're getting involved in," she said. "They weren't even friends with these guys before this. But all of a sudden, now that they're in jail, they're friends."

"It's a chance to socialize," Tony Miliotti's attorney Curtis Leftwich said. "There's a certain sexiness to the case." The danger and unexpected drama of it all shook up the monotonous lives of these suburban teens, like they had been plopped right into the middle of a big-screen thriller. The excitement of watching their former classmates and neighbors being tried for murder became addicting. Not just robbery, not assault, but murder. In their tiny, sleepy town. Leftwich explained that these spectators could not possibly embrace the reality of the situation just yet. For the time being, it all felt like a grand Shakespearean tragedy acted out on a stage. "Maybe later," he said, "when the trial gets started, they'll be more serious."

The article also added some background information on the players in the tragic story. Chris Velardo was painted as a sweet, quiet, impeccably dressed young man who generally "followed the crowd." Though he had attended the Indian Hills continuation school, he was never a discipline problem, and had transferred from the traditional high school because of truancy and falling grades. Chris was the main link between the two groups of boys involved in the fight, as he floated between the two. Described by friends and the school principal as an artistically gifted pretty boy, Chris had spent "most of his time crying" during the previous months, according to his attorney, Charles English. "He's genuinely remorseful for everything," English added.

The article also described Tony Miliotti as a quiet "follower" who attended Indian Hills continuation school with Chris and Jason. The three boys had been close friends since they were little. Abandoned by his mother when he was a small child, Tony had been raised partially by his father, but mostly by his aunt and uncle in Thousand Oaks. He enjoyed support from his large, tight-knit clan of extended family members, most of whom attended every court hearing. He was "totally nice, a gentleman," one acquaintance said. A tall, thin, strong boy with baby-blue eyes and a solid work ethic, Tony had worked since a young age, doing odd jobs and helping unload his uncle's produce trucks. Jason Holland often helped. Tony had no blemishes on his record.

The *LA Times* article was a little less kind to Jason and Micah Holland, essentially depicting them as a bit troubled. Sharry Holland told reporters that she had struggled to raise her boys in a safe environment, since their biological father had abandoned the family when the boys were only one and four years old. Both boys were labeled with attention deficit disorder, and Micah was described as "quick tempered" and having "a very big mouth" by neighbors and friends. At the end of the article it stated that Micah "claimed gang affiliation during the fight that left Jimmy Farris dead." The article also suggested that Jason had been involved in "receiving stolen property" when he was a juvenile, although that was not verified.

Although the Mary Pols article did not describe Brandon Hein or his background, it did add a few interesting details provided by a neighbor. Brandon Hein lived in a modest Oak Park condominium with his father, Gene, and Gene's fiancée, Janice. Phyllis Deikel lived next door. She reported to police that around three p.m. on the day Jimmy Farris died, she wandered out to her backyard and heard a ruckus behind the Hein residence. She said she heard an excited group of boys shouting, saying things like, "I can do it! You can't do it. You don't have the guts to do it." She went back into the house and told her husband, "Those boys are up to something." They could have been talking about anything, surfing a giant wave or skateboarding off a ramp, for all anybody knows. Still, her testimony in the October *LA Times* article planted tiny seeds of premeditation in the subconscious of the community.

Struggling to make sense of the crime and motive, police and the media leaked a little more information about the hours leading up to Jimmy's death. Mike McLoren's girlfriend, Stacey Williams, was featured on television often enough to provide her with her fifteen minutes of celebrity, and she was pegged as the media's darling, the expert on the case. Stacey described things from her perspective. Early in the day on May 22, Stacey said she, Chris Velardo's girlfriend, Natasha, Johnny Vinnedge, and John Berardis paid a day laborer to buy them beer at a local liquor store. They drank at her house for a while, then stumbled to Mike McLoren's fort. Mike and Jimmy arrived a bit later and they all smoked pot and watched Quentin Tarantino's *Pulp Fiction*. Johnny Vinnedge became so inebriated that he passed out on the fort's couch, and they all proceeded to draw with Sharpie pen on his stomach, naturally. The party lasted several hours. A few other friends wandered in and out, including Chris Velardo, who didn't stay long, presumably because he and Natasha were in a fight and the silent treatment became a bit awkward in the tiny fort gathering. Stacey, Natasha, and the two Johns had cleared out between six thirty and seven p.m., and returned to their families for dinnertime. Jimmy stayed inside the fort waiting while McLoren ran up to his kitchen and quickly ate some food with his mother and grandparents. When Mike returned to the fort after eating dinner, he realized that Stacey had "taken all the good weed" when she left. This explained why McLoren was so furious with his girlfriend that he had to work out his anger on the outside punching bag.

GANG LINK

IN JUNE 1995, A MONTH AFTER JIMMY FARRIS DIED, sixteen-year-old Taft High School student Ramtin Shaolian was shot and killed in front of the upscale Fallbrook Mall in nearby West Hills, California. Two teens, one nicknamed Ace Capone and the other Big Chocolate, claimed to be from a West Valley gang called Every Woman's Fantasy. Yes, they actually named themselves that. Truth is often stranger than fiction.

Apparently, Ramtin Shaolian and five friends were walking near the movie theater next to the mall, while these guys, Capone and Chocolate, were walking toward them, accompanied by four wealthy sixteen-year-old girls who had been drinking and smoking with them during the day. Mr. Chocolate asked Ramtin's group what gang they were from. When one of the six boys replied, "Do we look like gangbangers to you?" Chocolate took that as a sign of disrespect. He ordered Ace Capone and the four young girls to walk back toward his car, which was parked in the Fallbrook Mall parking lot.

Capone and Chocolate had no criminal records and were trying to impress the girls with their Wild West testosterone-fueled vengeance. The six teens piled into Big Chocolate's car and drove toward the movie theater. They stalked Ramtin's group, following closely behind, headlights off, until the boys approached the theater. Ace Capone pulled out a .22 pistol and fired a round of shots into the crowd, killing Ramtin Shaolian and severely wounding another boy. The four girls who'd accompanied Capone and Chocolate, who claimed no gang affiliation, nor any knowledge of a gun in the car, were initially charged with murder along with the "gang" boys. But eventually the girls were granted immunity in exchange for their testimony.

This gang, Every Woman's Fantasy (EWF), was also rumored to have been involved in another murder—the stabbing death of a fifteen-year-old Taft High School student named LaMoun Thames back in the summer of 1992, when he was heading home from preseason football practice. Two eighteen-year-old EWF boys were arrested and charged a couple of years later, after bragging to friends about committing the murder. Wannabe gang members often claim they've committed unsolved crimes in order to gain street cred from their peers. Fortunately for the two EWF kids, they never went to trial because all the witnesses had disappeared by then.

At some point in time, around early 1995, rumors swirled around town that it wasn't the EWF guys who had stabbed

LaMoun Thames, but rather a couple of members of the Gumbys. This was never validated. Still, the gossip spread, and the Gumbys were becoming something to be feared, at least mythologically speaking. The problem was that there were tagging crews and there were real gangs. The difference seemed to be that the former literally spent their time painting their names all over town as an act of local territorialism and rebellion, where real hardcore gangs—the Crips, the Bloods, 18th Street Gang, MS-13— were extremely organized and had sets all over the country, if not the world. They carried weapons, guns mainly, and made a lot of money through their entrepreneurial efforts. They ran businesses that were complex, if not legal. They had rules and rigid hierarchy systems with shot-callers, who gave orders to subordinates. The tagging crews were gang-lite, contemporary, and had names like WNA (We're No Angels), LIC (Like I Care), NSC (No Self-Control), and—yes—EWF. Once a kid claiming affiliation with a tagging group became violent and racked up a few murder charges, the whole crew was labeled as more of a gang, and consequently attracted attention from the FBI. This was a case of a bad apple or two spoiling the whole bunch.

Another *Los Angeles Times* article published on October 22, 1995, explained a little more about the gang link and suggested that the Gumbys were, in fact, venturing into more serious crime territory. But Los Angeles County Sheriff's Deputy Mike Berg, who worked with the juvenile intervention unit, described the Gumbys as a wannabe gang and laughed at the name, saying, "Pretty weak, huh? Like you'd want to be known as that."

He talked about the differences between loose wannabe cliques and real urban gangs, explaining that authentic gang members own and claim their affiliation, sporting tattoos, wearing colors or clothing specific to their gang. Their loyalty runs deep, often until death. The wannabes, however, like the Gumbys, don't have official colors, hand signs, or body art, mainly because they float in and out of groups and don't stick with them for very long.

Still, Micah's alleged statement right before the fight that ended in Jimmy Farris's death, "What, are you starting shit with Gumbys, *ese*?" was now published in public, and would be investigated, dissected, and repeated many times in the upcoming months, to the great detriment of Micah, Jason, Brandon, and Tony.

ESE

NOTHING HAPPENED IN THE CASE FOR ANOTHER four full months. On February 27, 1996, it was finally announced that jury selection was to begin for the trial of Case Number SA022108 in the Malibu Courthouse. The January trial date had come and gone. All anybody knew officially was that there were delays. Rumors spread that new evidence was being considered and that admissibility hearings were coming up. This meant that the prosecutors were pushing to admit something into the trial that the defense attorneys were trying to stop. February 28 also came and went, and still no jury was selected.

Finally, on March 19, 1996, the reasons for massive delays became apparent. For the next six days, Judge Mira listened to prosecutors Jeffrey Semow and his new partner, Michael Latin, argue with defense attorneys about whether to allow "evidence" that proved Jason, Micah, Brandon, and Tony were members of a gang. Showing this would not necessarily guarantee a jury would convict them of murder, but it would certainly strengthen the prosecution's case and add weight to the theory of them being hard-core criminals. Further, it would paint the four boys as really scary people, never a good feeling for a jury to have.

The testimony of the prosecution's "expert" witness on gang crimes included explanations of evidence that supposedly proved the boys were part of a gang. Officer Rollie Landtiser stated the first piece of evidence: Mike McLoren said he heard Micah Holland say "Gumbys" before the fight ensued. Second piece of evidence: an address book belonging to another boy who claimed to hang with the Gumbys. Brandon Hein's name and phone number were scrawled in the book. Next to Brandon's name was the word *Scarface*. Piece of evidence number three: a photograph of Brandon Hein in which he was wearing loose jeans that sagged below his waist. Exhibit number four: a photograph of Micah Holland's back. A cursive *M* was tattooed on the left shoulder, and a similar *H* on the right. Never mind that *M* and *H* were obviously Micah Holland's initials. Officer Landtiser said, "When you start putting things together . . . This is typical gangster, yes. I've seen this many times."

Rollie Landtiser also said he believed the Gumbys began as a dozen teens from North Hollywood who liked to go dancing together. Later, a group of friends called the Gremlins merged with the Gumbys, and they began tagging. Though there was no proof offered, he said that the two groups had recently been linked to real crimes like robbery and carjackings. "The

Gumbys have turned the corner," Landtiser declared.

Jason's trial attorney, Ira Salzman, said out loud what the other defense attorneys were thinking: "It's not proper expert testimony."

Brandon's attorney, Jill Lansing, reminded Judge Mira that baggy pants were all the rage in high schools across the country.

The best part of the evidentiary gang hearings was when Curtis Leftwich, Tony's attorney, asked Officer Landtiser, "Have you ever rendered an opinion on the Gumbys before?"

His response? "I didn't even know they existed until Thursday."

A Los Angeles Police Department gang expert who had never even heard of this particular gang? Perfect.

Judge Mira ruled all evidence provided by Officer Landtiser to be inadmissible. He insisted that Landtiser based his opinions on speculation and had no expertise on actions of the Gumbys. It felt like a massive point chalked up for the defense team. But then Mira decided that the jury could in fact hear very limited evidence. Though he ruled that prosecutors Semow and Latin could not say that the four defendants were members of the Gumbys, or talk about the photos, clothing, or Micah's tattoos, they could bring in experts to translate what Judge Mira called "gang terminology."

Micah's alleged statement, "What, are you starting shit with Gumbys, ese?" was all they had to go on. Mira ruled that the word ese was a Spanish slang term, unique only to gangs. Experts could be brought in to explain this during the trial. In reality, the term ese dates back to the 1940s and is Spanish for the letter *S*. Southerners—or Sureños—used it to address whomever they were speaking to. In the late 1960s the term did develop street gang connotations when Mexican-American gangs from Northern California battled with Southern sets, and the latter referred to themselves as Sureños. By the 1990s in the United States, however, using the term *ese* was similar to calling a friend "homie," "pal," "dog," "girlfriend," or "buddy."

First, there was no evidence that Micah had ever used the term *ese*, except for Mike McLoren's statement. Second, even if Micah had said *ese*, it was a common and trendy way to address friends and acquaintances at the time. Judge Mira most likely had not spent a lot of time outside the Malibu bubble and had no clue what the word *ese* meant.

MOUNTAIN PARK MURDER

ON MONDAY, MARCH 25, 1996, JUST AS THE Holland-Hein-Miliotti trial was finally getting under way, sixteen-year-old Will Futrelle lay bleeding to death on the dirt ground outside the boys' dormitory at the Mountain Park Baptist Boarding Academy two thousand miles away in Wayne County, Missouri. Will had been beaten in the head with a brick, his throat slashed twice. Three of his fellow students, eighteen-year-old Anthony Rutherford, fifteen-year-old Joseph Stanley Burris, and another fifteen-year-old classmate, admitted to killing Will in a rage.

For about three weeks, Will and his three friends had been plotting to steal hunting rifles from the teachers' and owners' stashes of weapons in an effort to take over the boarding school. They later claimed that they were fed up with the inhumane living conditions and brutal daily abuse allegedly at the hands of their guardians. Their plan was to hold the adults hostage until police and the media would be forced to infiltrate the campus. In his recorded twenty-two-minute statement to police, Anthony Rutherford told of his grand plan to have his way with some girls and perhaps start his own cult. "I was trying to overpower and take over, just push over Mountain Park in any way possible, so that I could start something, do things the way I wanted to do them . . . not be made to do something because it's the rules," Rutherford explained. He ended the statement by saying: "I felt like I was pushed around to a certain point. I was always looked down upon. I wanted to be looked up to." Later, during their trial, the boys said that they would have preferred prison or death over spending another day at Mountain Park, and stated that they'd assumed their plan would end with incarceration or suicide.

Will Futrelle had been a student at the residential school for only two months, and Joseph Burris was assigned as Will's mentor. According to the boys, Will grew conflicted about whether the plan would work and bailed out at the last minute. He told the others he was too scared to go through with it. Will said that he had "found God," then indicated that if the other boys initiated the plan, he'd feel compelled to tell on them. He said he didn't feel right about stealing. In a heated frenzy, they beat him up, hoping to shut him up.

The three boys later said the plan was to lead Will out into the woods and "basically beat the crap out of him." The attack began as a beating and escalated quickly. While the boys were out gathering firewood together, they grabbed Will and began pummeling him, first with their fists, then with a brick and a large hunk of wood resembling a club. "It was taking too long," Joseph Burris said during his recorded confession. "So I took a knife and cut his throat. He started wheezing and moving around, so I reached down and cut his throat open wider."

When the boys returned to their dorm, they immediately admitted what they had done. Investigators found the four-inch pocketknife, wooden club, and a brick lying next to Will's body. Sergeant L. W. Plunkett said, "All these guys are clean-cut American boys, very polite, and come from nice middle-class families. It's always incredible when people this age commit crimes like this."

The subsequent investigations into the Mountain Park Murder and a decade of abuse allegations brought to light some new mitigating circumstances regarding Jason and Micah Holland's behavior patterns since 1993. Just two years prior to Jimmy Farris's death, the Holland brothers had spent an entire year enrolled at Mountain Park Baptist Boarding Academy.

CRUEL AND UNUSUAL

ABANDONED BY THEIR OIL RIGGER FATHER IN NEW Orleans when Jason and Micah were only four and one, they grew up without any contact. By the time they were eight and five, Sharry had remarried and moved the family to California so their stepfather, Gary Holland, could find work as a sound engineer for television and movies. When Micah turned ten and Jason was thirteen, their thirty-five-year-old mother, Sharry, had another child with Gary. He loved baby Kylie. Sadly, it appears that love was something their stepfather had not shown the boys.

One of the earliest memories Micah recounts about his young life was an incident with Gary when the boy had just turned six. Reciting lines he had heard from the movie *Back to the Future*, he called Gary a "bastard." Gary sat Micah down and asked if he knew what that word meant. Micah did not. Still, because he was six and young children often say and do things inexplicably, he said he thought he knew what it meant. Micah was afraid of Gary. But Gary told Micah he would not hurt him, and that they were just going to have a talk about it, so he would never do that again. After a while, Micah relaxed, and realized he had dodged a beating. Just as he was letting Micah go on about his day, Gary turned to him and said, "You know how I said I wouldn't hit you? Yeah, well, you thought wrong. I'm still gonna beat you."

Micah maintained that Gary was often very calm and calculating like that. He wasn't necessarily a fly-off-the-handle type of guy who couldn't control his outbursts. He was insidious with his abuse, which was worse. Gary seemed to enjoy using sporadic beatings to try to keep the boys in line. He delighted in frightening them. He had always told Jason and Micah that this was the manner in which he was raised, and he "turned out just fine," a statement that is perhaps the most overused and clichéd reasoning imaginable.

Baby Kylie's addition to the family affected Micah in an unexpected way. Though he adored his little sister, witnessing the affection and kindness Gary Holland showered on Kylie, yet kept from the boys, created resentment. While Gary was sweet with Kylie in her first year of life, he either ignored the boys, beat them, or called them "little bastards" and "fucking nothings" constantly, according to Sharry. Micah began to act out. He got drunk for the first time at age ten. After enduring a massive hangover with vomiting and all the rest, he got up and repeated it the next day. He was hooked quickly. By age eleven, he was experimenting with hard stuff.

One day a crew of older boys from the neighborhood decided it was a good idea to bring Micah along to a party in Venice Beach to have some fun with another group of teens they knew—who several years later formed a Grammy Award–winning rap/metal band. Somebody urged Micah to smoke heroin, and from there his drug experimentation began. Drugs and alcohol provided an escape and numbed the pain caused by growing up in an unsafe, unpredictable environment.

In early 1992, unable to get a grip on twelve-year-old Micah through drug rehabilitation and counseling, Sharry decided she needed to do something drastic to whip him into shape. She and Gary had temporarily separated at this point, so she was working full-time as a real estate agent while raising her three children alone. She did not want to separate the boys, as they had always been extremely close. A family counselor suggested she look into sending them to boarding school. One in particular, Mountain Park Baptist Boarding Academy in southeast Missouri, looked strict yet serene and was within Sharry's budget. The tuition was $1200 per month for both boys. From what she could tell, it looked just like an old-fashioned summer camp, set deep in the lush woods a world away from the city. Remote and beautiful, Mountain Park Academy seemed the perfect solution to shield the boys from the bad influences in California.

Bob and Betty Wills were staunch "Christians" who had run the Bethesda Home for Girls in Hattiesburg, Mississippi, before closing it down amid lawsuits and allegations of child abuse and neglect. Specifically, they had been accused of beating and drugging pregnant teens. The Wills family was able to respond to a number of the charges with claims of "religious immunity." They were never convicted of any crimes in Mississippi. In 1987 "Mama" and "Papa" Wills opened the Mountain Park Academy, 180 acres of wilderness adjacent to the St. Francis River. Marketed as a rigid environment designed to set troubled youth straight, the academy's mission was to "separate teens from the ungodly." Desperate parents from all over the country sent their challenging teens to Mountain Park in the hopes of straightening them out. Using a combination of rigorous Bible instruction and corporal punishment, the academy boasted a "ninety percent success rate," whatever that meant. It's unclear what goals, objectives, and standards were established to measure their success.

In May of 1992, twelve-year-old Micah and fifteen-year-old Jason moved out to Missouri and enrolled in Mountain Park for an undetermined amount of time. According to Jason and Micah, the school had a harsh no-contact-with-family policy for new students. In fact, any access to the outside world was completely limited. Only after a few months of probation could students call home. And even then, calls were limited to once every few weeks and were monitored by the teachers, whom they were instructed to call "Brothers." Handwritten letters were also monitored and limited. Any complaints about the school or administration were literally blacked out of the pages.

Upon entering the school, the boys were assigned mentors, seasoned students who had paid their dues and accepted Christ and the academy's teachings as the word of God. Each mentor was expected to remain within what they called "slapping distance" of his protégé during the months of the probation period. During this time, new kids could not make eye contact with older students, were not allowed to express emotions like sadness or fear, and certainly could not cry. They were prevented from complaining or speaking about their past in any way. This meant no discussion of home, family, former friends, or any experiences they'd had prior to entering Mountain Park. This was all spelled out in their handbook, and seemed to be their method of wiping the slate clean. Students were not permitted to see their parents for one full year.

Although it was a bizarre environment, Jason and Micah initially enjoyed the camaraderie with other boys and exposure to the outdoors. Boys slept in cabins with bunk beds, much like the sleepaway summer camp they had envisioned. Between sessions of studying scripture in silence, they were able to paddle canoes, ride horses, and play sports. They swam and hiked a lot. They reveled in actually finding ways to have good, wholesome fun without the influences of drugs or alcohol.

But Mountain Park had a dark side, one that in no way resembled summer camp. According to the Brothers, animals were completely insignificant. They "had no souls" was what they said. Jason and Micah were enormous animal lovers, who had spent their only good days with their stepfather, Gary, helping him film and edit footage of dolphins and whales for Jacques Cousteau's television documentaries. One thing that impressed them the most was how majestic and intelligent sea animals were. They could feel emotions and actually talk to one another! Micah wasn't buying this whole foolish story about animals having no souls. To his horror, he watched as the Brothers "proved it" to him by pulling out shotguns, then methodically shooting dead a group of dogs that roamed the school campus.

The boys could also be whacked with giant wooden rackets for infractions ranging from crying about missing home to refusing to recite scripture. The Mountain Park staff members later admitted using these techniques, but indicated they used them sparingly, only after "talking through" the violations with the boys failed to work. However, according to multiple former students, beatings were frequent, yet unreliable and senseless, rules changing from one day to the next. Also, according to Micah and several former students, if two or more boys had an argument, they were forced by the Brothers to fight it out, gladiator style, like a scene out of some sick torture film. The Brothers would gather the others in a circle, toss the offenders into the middle, and instruct them to fight until all involved were bruised and bloodied and somebody gave up. Micah described it as living in a real-life *Lord of the Flies*.

Jason described Mountain Park Baptist Boarding Academy as "just eerie." Although high fences topped with barbed razor wire surrounded the school, Jason managed to escape three different times. At one point, he ran away from Mountain Park with another boy and they made it pretty far on foot. They were soaking wet and cold after trudging through dewy meadows for a few hours, so they stopped at a small bait-and-tackle shop to warm up. When they asked a customer if she had any cigarettes, she quickly called her brother, who *was* one of the Mountain Park Brothers. Jason and his friend were promptly rounded up and brought back to the campus. The third time he escaped, he was found by Brothers, who had tracked him down on horseback. He was then forced to sleep with no clothing or pajamas on or near him to prevent him from escaping again.

Sharry said that around Christmastime of that year, she could tell by reading their letters that Jason and Micah had changed, and not for the better. Stories of Brothers killing animals in front of the boys and lectures given by the staff describing homosexuals as perverts that needed to be exterminated disturbed her. The boys seemed to have become brainwashed, she said. After having been enrolled at Mountain Park for an entire year, in May 1993 the boys came home for a visit and ended up staying home.

Unfortunately, Mountain Park was not an accredited American school. Because their religious studies classes (the only classes they were allowed to take) did not transfer to the California public school system, both Jason and Micah had fallen well behind their classmates upon returning home. Eventually, Jason quit school altogether and planned to study for the GED. School was undoubtedly awkward for Micah at that time as well—he was a year older but one year behind his friends.

During the next six months, Jason and Micah were inseparable. Sharry said that Jason seemed to be incredibly protective of Micah, and she surmised that her older son had spent the entire previous year taking care of his brother as both bodyguard and father figure. Things heated up when Sharry reconciled with Gary Holland, and she and her children moved back in with him. In spring of 1995, Gary beat Jason so badly, he broke his nose.

Nobody knew what exactly went down at Mountain Park when Jason and Micah Holland attended, but many others have certainly described an oppressive environment consistent with what Jason and Micah reported. Again, there was no widely used Internet back in 1992, and certainly no cell phones or social media. Worse, the State of Missouri had a hands-off policy when it came to private schools, particularly those with religious foundations. Neither the state's Department of Education nor the Department of Social Services oversaw the school. This certainly may explain why Bob and Betty Wills moved their operation from Mississippi to Missouri.

The Mountain Park Baptist Boarding Academy was shut down in 2004. The owners and staff faced lawsuits and numerous reports of abuse over the subsequent years. Former students filed lawsuits claiming damages from assault, battery, false imprisonment, denial of medical treatment to minors, intentional infliction of emotional distress, and improper administration of various tranquilizers and antipsychotic drugs. However, the Wills family never faced any criminal charges, and they have always defended their approaches to disciplining children.

Since 2004, dozens of people who had been enrolled at Mountain Park throughout the years have been commiserating on websites and message boards, trading horror stories of abuse and neglect and detailing the post-traumatic stress disorder symptoms many still carry with them. They call themselves the Mountain Park Survivors. Much of their frustration lies in the fact that their parents had signed over guardianship for the duration of matriculation. Because communication with families was severely limited, and monitored when there was contact, these teens felt they were unable to tell anybody in the outside world what was really happening. Their voices were taken away. One former student, who has remained very vocal over the years, referred to Mountain Park Academy as a "compound of horrors."

Regardless of what the truth is about Mountain Park Baptist Boarding Academy, it's safe to say that at a critical time in their development Jason and Micah Holland found themselves in a highly controversial placement for wayward youth, which used questionable practices to keep them in line. Such practices appeared to have made sure they saw violence as an appropriate response to a threat.

TRIAL

ON THE COOL, BREEZY MORNING OF TUESDAY, March 26, 1996, Brandon and Tony were led into the Malibu courthouse wearing collared shirts and ties. Jason wore a tweed blazer, and Micah a white sweater. Friends and family of the Farrises crammed into one side of the room, and supporters of the Hollands, Heins, and Miliottis filled the other. Sharry Holland later told Randall Sullivan, of *Rolling Stone*, that Judge Mira "seemed to hate these boys from the first moment he looked at them" that morning.

Before the jury was led into the courtroom, the defense and prosecution teams had a heated debate regarding which photographs should be plastered around the courtroom. Specifically, the defense attorneys objected to the use of unflattering images of their defendants. The pictures of Jason, Micah, Brandon, and Tony were mug shots that literally depicted them as filthy, unkempt thugs with scowls on their faces. The giant photos of Jimmy Farris and Mike McLoren, on the other hand, showed clean young men smiling and posing in brightly colored shirts. After a couple of hours of back-and-forth, Judge Mira finally ruled that the pictures of the defendants were not prejudicial or pejorative. The giant photographs, which seemed to send a clear message to the jurors—*this is a battle of good versus evil*—would stay.

When Judge Mira asked if there was anything else that needed to be handled before they finally brought the jury in, prosecutor Semow nonchalantly said, "While they were sitting here going over the photographs with Mr. Latin, I was setting up the tape recorder. I'm going to play the 911 tape regarding the stabbing to the jury in my opening statement." Generally speaking, emergency 911 recordings fall under the hearsay rule and are therefore not admissible as evidence in a trial. *Hearsay* is the legal term for statements that were made out of court that someone is trying to use as proof of a truth. There are dozens of complicated exceptions to the hearsay rule—so many, in fact, that evidence courses in American law schools dedicate much of their time to examining this tiny piece of the law. Jill Lansing argued that there was no such applicable exception in this case, and no reason to play the tape. Further, the discussion on the 911 recording between Nancy McLoren and the dispatch operator was completely irrelevant, because every bit of that information was to be presented during the trial when questioning witnesses. Normally, judges uphold the hearsay rule in these cases and forbid the playing of 911 recordings. However, after much discussion and argument between the opposing teams, without any explanation, an exhausted Judge Mira declared, "All right. I will overrule the objection. Use the tape."

The jury members, five men and seven women, were led into the courtroom. Judge Mira told them that Mr. Semow was going to begin with his opening statement, and explained that this statement was only an outline of what was to be presented during the trial. The jury members were instructed to listen without taking notes. "An opening statement is not evidence," Judge Mira reminded them. "Neither is it an argument. Counsel are not permitted to argue the case at this point." Even though the jury members were told that they could not consider what they were about to hear as evidence, there was no way anyone could possibly unhear the emotional exchange on the recording.

Jeffrey Semow walked toward the jury box. He stood before the jurors, and then he paused for a few seconds. "Ladies and gentlemen, I want you to listen to something." He pressed play. The 911 recording of Nancy McLoren shouting at the dispatch operator was painfully sad. She and her mother, Georgette, could be heard in the most heightened state of panic. They screamed and begged for immediate help, while the operator calmly instructed them to apply towels to the wounds. Their voices revealed the terror running through their bodies as they tried unsuccessfully to stop the bleeding from Jimmy's chest. Mrs. McLoren kept repeating, "They've been stabbed! This one's bleeding all over the place. Send somebody. Send somebody!"

Jim and Judie Farris both cried and hugged while the recording played. Jason, Micah, Brandon, and Tony all stared down at the tables in front of them. Audible gasps came from the jury box. Finally Mr. Semow pressed stop. "Ladies and gentlemen, that was Nancy McLoren." Semow pointed to a giant poster of Jimmy Farris with a wide, braces-filled smile that was attached to the back wall of the courtroom. "He stopped breathing very shortly after that phone call was made." The choice to open the trial on such a powerfully gut-wrenching note was brilliant, and no doubt etched the pain of the McLoren and Farris families into the memories of the jurors. It set the tone for the prosecution's case perfectly.

Jeffrey Semow spent more than an hour presenting an outline of the prosecution's evidence. He said the four defendants were "menacing bullies" who clearly drove to Mike McLoren's home on May 22, 1995, to steal from him. He insisted that the two groups of boys were basically strangers. According to Semow, the two crews knew of each other only because they shared one friend in common, Chris Velardo. Chris's girlfriend, Natasha, was close with Mike McLoren's girlfriend, Stacey. On this afternoon these four boys had invaded Mike's "little zone of privacy" without invitation. He told the jury that later they would hear that Micah Holland had visited the McLoren fort on occasion in the past. However, he instructed them not to interpret that as a friendship. No, Mike McLoren had only allowed Micah to come over and smoke pot on previous occasions because McLoren was "afraid of Micah."

Semow was careful to describe Jimmy Farris and Mike McLoren as completely dissimilar personalities. Jimmy was "extroverted, well-adjusted, an outdoorsman who was close to both his parents, but independent at the same time." Mike, on the other hand, was described as "having some problems" mainly because he liked to smoke a lot of pot. Mike had named an accomplice to police when he was arrested a few years prior for stealing a police officer's gun, Semow continued. After that, other kids "made his life hell." Specifically, "Micah made his life hell."

None of the four defense attorneys provided opening statements. Generally, it should be a defense strategy to win over a jury from the first minute. In this case, it would seem to have been especially smart for them to provide opening statements, at least to diffuse the intensity of the prosecution's opening. On rare occasions, defense teams will opt out of delivering opening statements, usually because they are unsure of what surprises lurk around the corner. In this case it would appear all the discovery was shared among the attorneys, and there was nothing new as far as anybody knew. Why the four defense attorneys chose not to offer opening statements on behalf of their clients remains a mystery.

WITNESSES

ON WEDNESDAY, MARCH 27, MICHAEL LATIN, SEMOW'S new partner from the district attorney's office, called the prosecution's first witness. Latin was young and hungry to launch his career, and he reveled in the opportunity to try such a newsworthy case. A small, handsome man with sandy hair and deer-in-the-headlights wide eyes, Latin had a soothing voice and chose his words carefully. His calm demeanor was a welcome contrast to the gruff Semow, who had dominated the case so far.

John Berardis was the first witness. Friends with all seven boys involved, on that Monday, May 22, Berardis had ditched his Indian Hills continuation school classes for the day with three of his classmates. Because Stacey had keys to the fort, she took Berardis, Johnny Vinnedge, and Natasha Sinkinson to spend the day partying over there. According to Berardis, Mike McLoren and Jimmy Farris stopped by at lunchtime to take a few hits of marijuana off the bong, then went back to class at their school, Agoura High, which was only three blocks away. They returned at 2:35 p.m., after school was out.

It seemed that the prosecution needed Mr. Berardis to establish several things. First, since Mike and Jimmy had not been there as long as the others, they wanted to show that the two probably weren't very impaired. Second, although the other five ditched school to get drunk and high that day, Mr. Latin tried to establish that they had only smoked the "weak stuff" and therefore could probably remember everything pretty solidly. This became important, because it was suggested that Natasha Sinkinson had gone out to Stacey's car to locate her wallet at one point in the day. That was allegedly the same time that her boyfriend, Chris Velardo, showed up for a few minutes. They needed this information to establish a timeline, among other accusations that would soon become apparent. Semow and Latin were also trying to show that their witnesses were credible and not "too high" or "too drunk" and everything they were saying was accurate.

Upon cross-examination, or when attorneys for the defense questioned Berardis, they tried really hard to paint him and his friends as sort of low-life druggies who weren't very bright, nor did they have any respect for their education or the law. The problem with heated trials like this one is that witnesses, who are doing their civic duty, are interrogated as if they are on trial for committing the crimes. After hammering away at John Berardis regarding the illegality of drinking underage, one of the defense attorneys questioned him about how they got the beer that day.

"We just had Natasha flag down some Mexican dude. And he bought us the beer. There was some Mexican dude, like, at Jack in the Box, so we went there, and we like told him to meet us like at Burger King right next to the thing [Party Time Liquor], and then he brought the beers in a bag." When attorney Leftwich asked, "Have you done this before, got a Mexican dude to buy beer for you?" Berardis replied, "Yes."

The attorneys for the prosecution and the defense went back and forth with John Berardis all day long, one side trying to paint him and his friends as honest and credible, the other tearing that opinion down. At one point prosecutor Michael Latin began a lengthy discussion of the difference between "good weed" and "bad weed" and the effects of each and how marijuana is different from alcohol. Latin was trying to prove that since Jimmy and Mike had smoked "weak" pot that day with the others, they could not have been amped up or ready for a fight. This was based on John Berardis suggesting that "bad weed" makes people tired. "It's just like if you smoke cheap—like dirty—like not good stuff, you might be stoned like ten minutes or something, and then you'll just be like a vegetable, you know? Like, tired." Prosecutor Latin was trying to lead him to say that they had all, in fact, only smoked the cheap stuff. John Berardis didn't comply.

Poor Berardis couldn't remember if they had smoked good stuff or bad stuff, or how tired or fired up any of them were. In fact, the discussion became so incredibly detailed and hilarious, Berardis finally tossed up his hands in exasperation. "You've never smoked weed?! You don't know what . . . Jesus!"

Latin responded with a lengthy blank stare. "Have you ever met anybody that doesn't smoke weed?"

"No. Yeah. I don't know." Berardis shrugged. "Older people, I guess."

"Like me?"

"Yeah."

"First time for everything."

The testimony and cross-examination of John Berardis became a mind-numbing jumble of repeating the same information in dozens of different ways. An entire day seemed to have been wasted on minutiae that didn't help either side. Starting off on this note suggested that the rest of the trial would be just as slow.

The next day the prosecution called Natasha Sinkinson, Chris Velardo's girlfriend, as their second witness. Natasha bounced up to the witness stand, full of cool hippie vibes, with natural blond curls and a cherub face. She testified for two full days, describing the details of the small party in the fort. Natasha knew all seven boys involved and testified that, yes, she and her three friends had ditched school that day to party in Mike McLoren's fort. This involved drinking and smoking a lot of marijuana. She stated that she and Johnny Vinnedge drank most of the assortment of giant forty-ounce bottles of beer, and that they were both very drunk.

Natasha described walking out to Stacey's car sometime

between three and four p.m. to find her wallet. At that time she saw Chris pulling up in his red truck. She watched him exit the truck and hop over the McLoren fence, then walk down to the fort. She did not acknowledge him, because they were in a fight and not speaking to each other. She went back and forth about thinking she saw other people sitting inside the truck, but she could not identify how many or who they were. She thought she saw shaved heads. The prosecution tried mightily to lead her to identify the others in the truck based on seeing the backs of their heads. Michael Latin pounded away at the fact that she should absolutely have known what the back of Jason Holland's head looked like. After all, she had dated him two years ago, hadn't she? How many times had she seen the back of Brandon Hein's head? Hadn't she been "hanging out" with Brandon the last couple of weeks before Jimmy's death because she was mad at her boyfriend, Chris?

Although this proved nothing, the prosecutors used her story to show that the crew of five boys might have been "casing the joint" in the hours before the attack. This added to their theory that the event was a robbery. Ira Salzman, Jason's attorney, of course questioned Natasha's credibility, reminding the jury that she was drunk and very high during the hours about which she was testifying. Natasha Sinkinson's testimony failed the prosecution. She was inconsistent, spacey, and clearly could not remember most of the details of the day. Neither Natasha nor John Berardis had any clue what day of the week this had occurred. Wouldn't the homicide of a good friend mark a day that was somewhat etched in someone's head?

Next-door neighbor Barbara Wampler was called to the stand next. She stated that she had seen the boys in the maroon truck sitting outside the McLoren home at exactly five p.m. She explained that she was exactly "forty-three feet away from the truck" and could clearly see and identify Jason, Brandon, and Micah, even though she had never seen any of those boys before. She said she noticed the boys were "jumpy, nervous," and craning their necks to see down toward the fort. She said that all three sat in the cab of the truck, and nobody got out. She also claimed that when the truck driver saw her watching and sped away, he hit another neighbor's metal trash can, making a loud noise. Strangely, Jimmy, Mike, and John Berardis had remembered hearing Chris hit the trash can when he had left earlier, between three and four. This detail illustrated an important point. Witness testimony is never 100 percent accurate. Memories are plastic and change over time, depending on what people have read or heard about certain cases. It is possible that Barbara Wampler saw Chris Velardo pull up in his truck between three and four o'clock but was confused about the time. It's possible that she never saw Jason, Micah, and Brandon in the truck at that time, but her memory filled that piece in after reading so much about the case. Also, it came out later that Wampler's husband was a sergeant with the Los Angeles Police Department. Therefore, it was suggested by some that perhaps she had not seen the boys scoping out the McLoren fort that day but wanted to help the prosecution's case.

* * *

At one point, after a week or so had passed, Jill Lansing approached Judge Mira to let him know that her client, Brandon, was not receiving hot meals; nor was he allowed to shower on trial days. The other defense attorneys chimed in and stated the same. These claims were never investigated, and it could only be speculated that people in the system were messing with the four boys on purpose. Also, during jury recess and lunch breaks, the boys were forced to stand for hours at a time in separate little storerooms with no access to chairs, water, or bathroom facilities. When the defense lawyers complained about this, they were told there was nothing that could be done. The Malibu Courthouse was tiny, not equipped to hold more than one or two defendants at a time, and none of the four boys could be anywhere near each other. Needless to say, it was a long and uncomfortable nine weeks for Jason, Brandon, Micah, and Tony.

On Wednesday, April 3, Jeffrey Semow called Alyce Moulder to the stand. She described how she had been playing with her six-month-old baby and two-year-old toddler at Gates Canyon Park when she watched the boys in the maroon truck pull into the empty parking lot. She watched one jump out, open her passenger door, and take her wallet off the front dashboard. She yelled, "Don't take my wallet! It has my license in it." Alyce and her two children had recently become homeless and were staying with friends in the area until they got back on their feet. All she could think about was that she had no money to get to the DMV to apply for a new driver's license. She said she heard the boys laughing before they sped off and turned right out of the parking lot.

Alyce scooped up her children, placed them into their car seats, and exited the park, turning right onto Thousand Oaks Boulevard. She pulled into a small strip mall just down the street, hoping to catch the truck full of boys. She spotted the truck in the mall parking lot. The driver sat up front alone. Alyce left her children and dog in her van, ran over, opened Chris Velardo's passenger door, and grabbed him by the neck. When she shook him and told him to give her wallet back, he repeated, "I don't have your wallet. I don't have your wallet." Soon after, she saw four other boys approach the truck. According to her, one boy took a Club (a two-foot-long metal device used to lock up steering wheels before car alarms were standard) out of the truck bed, held it up, and threatened her with it. He said, "You'd better get out of here, homegirl, or I will mess you up."

She retreated to her van, started up the engine, then purposely gunned it backward toward the boys to scare them, stopping only a couple of feet from where they stood. According to Ms. Moulder, the boys pounded on the windows and kicked her car. One spit on the front window. As she drove away, one of the boys picked up rocks and threw them at her car. When asked who that was, she replied that it was "one of the short ones with a skinhead." She thought it was Brandon, then maybe Micah. But since they looked so similar at the time, she couldn't be sure. Also, she was looking in the side-view mirror as she drove away, and thought they had thrown rocks, but didn't actually see them.

The jury was instructed that, by law, they could not use the Alyce Moulder Incident to judge the boys or label them as "bad" people or "criminals." After all, they were not on trial for stealing a wallet. The story could be used only for background, and when considering intent with respect to the killing of Jimmy Farris. Regardless, it didn't much matter what they were or were not supposed to judge. Alyce Moulder's testimony was powerful and really appealed to the jurors' emotions. It was a genius maneuver on the part of the prosecution, because it created images in the jurors' heads that could not be erased. How could they not judge Jason, Brandon, Micah, and Tony unfavorably after that?

The next couple of weeks were slow and painful. The trial took a full week hiatus so that one of the defense attorneys could attend a planned family vacation. On Tuesday, April 16, the trial continued with Stacey Williams's testimony. She described how she and her friends often played video games, watched movies, and smoked pot and drank while visiting her boyfriend Mike's fort. She had known Mike, Jimmy, the Holland brothers, Chris, and Tony for many years. But Brandon was newer to the area. Micah had partied with Mike, Stacey, and Jimmy in the fort several times over the last year without incident. Stacey described spending every single day for the past year or so getting high with Mike in the fort. Strangely, she said that the kids coming and going would often have to sneak around to get into the fort. Mike didn't want people climbing over the fence, because then his grandparents—who were always home—could see people coming and going. "We were afraid of his parents," Stacey said, referring to his mother and grandparents. But once they were inside the fort, nobody bothered them.

Stacey said that on that Monday, May 22, 1995, she and her friends were very drunk and high, watching *Pulp Fiction* and *Natural Born Killers*. Around five p.m. she, Natasha, and John Berardis decided to drive Johnny Vinnedge home because he was inebriated and needed to get to bed. They then drove to a nearby park to purchase sixty dollars' worth of "kind bud," because it was a superior grade "endo" and provided a much better high than the "sins" they had smoked all day. They brought it back to the fort and the five friends smoked "bong loads" together. Everybody except Mike and Jimmy cleared out and went home to their families for dinnertime just before seven p.m.

At one point Stacey tried to downplay the role of drugs in their lives. But then she admitted that smoking was a social thing they all did on a regular basis. Every single day, actually. She seemed to have forgotten that she had admitted that only minutes before. Further, she explained that she and McLoren always shared his pot stashes with friends visiting the fort. Oh, and why had Mike kept Baggies of marijuana in the locked drawer of the desk? Stacey answered matter-of-factly that other kids who were not regular visitors, mostly acquaintances, came to purchase the marijuana. Mike usually sold quantities of eighths, the equivalent of 3.5 grams, or one large joint. He sold to various people, every day that she'd known him for the last couple of years. That was why it was all separated into small Baggies. Eventually, during her long and tedious testimony, Stacey admitted that she and Mike both sold drugs regularly to "afford their habit."

Although Mike McLoren had previously claimed that he'd

never sold drugs, Stacey added, "On occasion what would happen is, like, we'd hook up our friends, you know, and we wouldn't, like, they'd get it or whatever. But, like, little kids, you know, sometimes you don't give them as much as you should, and then you make a little bit of profit." So, not only did Mike and Stacey sell drugs on a daily basis to friends and acquaintances, they scalped to "little kids" who paid more because they didn't know any better and were desperate to get high.

When Jill Lansing cross-examined Stacey, she admitted that she had no reservations about confessing this information. Why? Because even though she was currently on probation for possessing and selling drugs, among other things, the prosecution had given her immunity for her testimony. This meant that no matter what she admitted to on the stand, she could never get into trouble or be prosecuted for breaking any laws because she was helping the prosecution with their case. Immunity is often granted by the state to witnesses who can strengthen a case; as a result, back-door promises and shady deals can often operate behind the scenes during criminal trials.

This seemed like very bad news for Mike McLoren, who had gone on record with the police insisting he never sold drugs. He was set to take the stand the very next day. Ironically, Mike's having been a drug dealer worked to his and the prosecution's great advantage in the end.

MIKE VERSUS JASON

MIKE

MIKE MCLOREN TOOK THE WITNESS STAND ON Wednesday, April 17, as the state's star and only witness to the crime. The entire case hinged on his credibility and how the jury perceived him. Dressed in a dark gray suit, crisp white shirt, and red tie, Mike appeared to have aged quite a few years in the previous eleven months. His dark hair was slicked back, showcasing his glassy eyes and dark circles beneath them.

While recounting the story, McLoren admitted that he had smoked marijuana with his friends on the afternoon of May 22, 1995. He also expressed his anger at his girlfriend, Stacey, because when she left she took "all the stuff that was good," referring to the "kind bud" or potent "endo." That was why he was taking out his aggression on the punching bag when Micah, Tony, Brandon, and Jason showed up. Mike's story was something of a disaster. Although he remembered that Micah took the lead and entered the fort ahead of the other boys, he could not answer the question about who threw the first punch.

When Michael Latin asked him what happened first inside the fort, McLoren remembered Micah saying, "Gimme the keys, fool."

"What words did you hear after Micah said, 'Gimme the keys, fool'?"

"'You want shit with Gumbys, *ese*?'"

"*Ese*? Is that a word you've heard before?"

"Yes."

"Gumbys. Is that a word you've heard before?"

"Yes."

"Did that statement have an effect on you?"

"A little bit."

"What effect did it have on you?"

"Intimidated me a little more."

"Why?"

"Because it's a gang. You know? Gangs are problems!"

"Do you know what *ese* means?"

"It's a Mexican slang term. It's used before a fight ensues."

It was the exact wording Judge Mira had used in the pretrial hearings regarding the gang issue. There is no doubt that prosecutors Semow and Latin prepped McLoren to use those same words.

Then McLoren gleefully described how he overpowered Micah Holland, threw him down on the bed, then jabbed him repeatedly with elbow blows to the back of his head. The problem for Micah at this point in the trial was that the jury was now looking at a sixteen-year-old boy who, in the eleven months prior to the trial, had gone through a major adolescent growth spurt. The young boy who Mike McLoren beat up had stood just over five feet tall and weighed barely more than one hundred pounds. Now sitting in the courtroom was Micah Holland approaching manhood, half a foot taller and more than twenty-five pounds heavier. It would have been impossible for the jury members to fathom the inequity of the fight.

Mike could place Micah, Brandon, and Jason inside the fort. When asked about Tony Miliotti, he said, "Tony was like in the doorway. He wasn't in it [the fort], but he wasn't not in it. He was in the doorway." He couldn't recall if Tony had touched anybody. When asked if he was scared when the three boys entered his fort asking for the keys to his marijuana drawer, he answered, "No." When asked "Why?" McLoren said, "Because I had Jim."

When probed about his history, and Jimmy protecting him, Mike explained that he had gotten into about "thirty or so" fights in the last few years. His troubles began three years before, when he and a friend burglarized the home of a police officer. McLoren was only in eighth grade. They had stolen a gun, and Mike sat on it for more than a month before the police caught up to him and brought him in for questioning. He lied to them about the event and claimed it wasn't him. But they had evidence and they pressed him. They would eventually drop the charges, but only if he gave up his crime partner, who happened to be an eighteen-year-old named Dave Wiley. The same Dave Wiley who coined the term *Gremlins*. Well-known and liked throughout Agoura Hills, Wiley had a lot of friends. And he clearly could not let it go. The crews in the valley did not take kindly to snitches.

When McLoren showed up on the first day of his freshman year at Agoura High School, he described being greeted by "about eighty people" who chased, surrounded, then attacked him. He avoided school for a while. Jimmy and Mike had been best friends for eight years, and Jimmy had a fierce protective streak. Jimmy Farris was loyal and kept McLoren out of a lot of binds, because nobody would mess with him. For the next couple of years, Mike was assaulted only when he was alone. Still, he grew tired of it. After he'd suffered relentless teasing for being a "narc," Jimmy suggested he buff up and taught him to fight.

Mike McLoren continued. "Jason runs at me, because I'm beating up Micah . . . so I kick him right in the face, and he goes back screaming, holding his nose." He said that after he kicked Jason, "my eyes were, like, being covered with clothes and stuff." The remainder of Mike's story was a lot of speculation about what might have happened. He said he was pulled off in a headlock, but he couldn't say by whom. He thought Jimmy was sitting on the couch being punched but, again, couldn't identify the perpetrator. Spectators in the courtroom remember prosecutors Semow and Latin literally cringing at some of the things Mike McLoren was saying. "Jim was an animal, really muscular. Nobody could compete with Jim!" At one point Mike pointed out that Jimmy Farris had always carried a pocketknife with him. Little of his testimony seemed to add to the prosecution's case.

The prosecution switched direction. They instructed McLoren to describe exactly what happened after he and Jimmy ran into the kitchen. Jimmy ran in first and crashed right onto the kitchen table. He sat in a chair and rested his head on the table. Nancy McLoren, her parents, and her sister all ran in to help. Mike McLoren told them they had been stabbed. He was jumping around, and in his agitated state told his mother to go outside and lock up his fort immediately. She complied. "I didn't want anybody to take my stuff," he said.

When she returned, Nancy called 911, then juggled trying to hold Jimmy upright and talk on the phone at the same time. After noticing blood pooling on Jimmy's shirt around his stomach, she screamed at the emergency operator to send people. The dispatcher told her to have the boys lie on the floor with their feet up on chairs. Nancy McLoren lay down with Jimmy while her mother, Georgette Thille, took the phone. "Apply pressure to the wounds!" Georgette relayed. Mike lay next to Jimmy on the floor and heard him struggling to breathe. Georgette then called Judie Farris. Jimmy made gurgling sounds. Nancy McLoren held Jimmy's hand and kept repeating, "I'm here. It's okay." Jimmy looked her in the eyes and said, "Mom." Then he stopped breathing. Judie Farris ran into the kitchen at that moment.

Prosecutors Semow and Latin concluded their direct examination of McLoren by having him lift up his shirt for the jury to reveal his battle scars. He showed them two one-inch-long scars on his back and a large vertical scar running down his front right side. He explained that the scar was from the surgery where physicians cut away at his stomach to mend his liver and put tubes into his collapsed lung to reinflate it.

Thursday's cross-examination by the defense team didn't play very well for Mike McLoren. Tony Miliotti's defense attorney, Curtis Leftwich, stated, "This is a young man who was ready for a fight." The defense attorneys painted Mike as a lying, conniving drug dealer. After all, he had lied to police when he initially described the incident as being an attempt to steal his television and VCR. He had insisted he did not deal drugs and possessed only small amounts of pot for him and his friends to smoke. Under intense questioning, Mike finally admitted that, yes, he did sell marijuana to other teens. When pressed, he guessed maybe thirty or so. Why had he lied initially? they asked. Because he was afraid he would get into trouble for selling pot.

As for his drug usage? He only smoked before school. And during lunch breaks. And after school. It wasn't his affinity for marijuana that they were criticizing. Rather, they were trying to make a point, emphasizing that a boy who was that high that often, and certainly on the evening in question, would have difficulty recalling details of events properly. When Curtis Leftwich played audio portions of McLoren's May 26 interview with detectives Tauson and Neumann, the jury heard Mike admit, "My mind sort of confused me. It's all sort of vague."

Smoking even small amounts of marijuana has serious effects on the human brain. Specifically, transferring memories from short-term to long-term is extremely difficult. People under the influence often forget thoughts midsentence and have trouble sustaining a lengthy conversation. A brand-new memory generally has to stick for fifteen to thirty seconds for it to have the opportunity to become processed into the long-term memory system. The problem for Mike McLoren was that he smoked so much marijuana on the afternoon of May 22, it would have been nearly impossible for him to process and remember details, especially one year later.

When asked by Jason's defense attorney, Ira Salzman, about his obvious smoking session just prior to testifying at a January 4 hearing, Mike replied, "I didn't *feel* high." Claiming under oath that you'd been smoking marijuana just minutes before appearing at a courthouse hearing, for a murder trial no less, can never look good in the eyes of the jury. Although Mike McLoren was not on trial for murder, the entire case rested on his credibility. There is no doubt his flippant attitude began to sour the opinions of jurors.

Jim Sussman, Micah Holland's trial attorney, wrapped up the day with his questioning of McLoren. It was his theory that Mike McLoren had actually started the fight, not Micah. Although the prosecution had presented the story as if the two groups of boys were strangers, that wasn't actually the case. The truth was that Micah was friends with Mike McLoren and Jimmy Farris. So was Brandon Hein. They all liked one another and had never had an incident. And not long before the evening of the fight, Micah attended a sleepover at McLoren's house. When all the boys were at another friend's house for a party, a group of teens had been

making fun of McLoren for being kind of a "poser" and a "wimp."
They teased that the only reason people didn't mess with Mike
anymore was because he had Jimmy as his "muscle." Jimmy was
well liked and strong, so by association it helped Mike's reputation tremendously, especially after the Dave Wiley incident.
During this particular party, about a week before the fort brawl,
Mike had felt "burned" by Micah when he left to smoke and party
with the guys who were clowning on McLoren.

Jim Sussman avoided beating around the bush when questioning McLoren. "You are a thief and a drug dealer, are you
not?" He repeated back what Mike had described about holding
Micah down and elbowing the back of his neck.

Sussman: Were you trying to break his neck?

McLoren: No. I was trying to hurt him. But not break his
neck.

Sussman: You were trying to break his neck. You were in a
rage.

MIKE VERSUS JASON

JASON

ON MONDAY, APRIL 29, THE ENTIRE COURTROOM WAS shocked to see Ira Salzman call his witness, Jason Holland, to take the stand. In murder trials, it is often defense strategy to avoid putting defendants up into the witness box. The shredding from prosecutors can often be so brutal, it sways a jury to strongly dislike the defendant.

When asked to describe all the events he could remember from May 22, 1995, Jason started by telling the jury he'd woken up at noon, then eaten breakfast. He got a ride from his friend Katy Anderson over to his friend Dwayne Dahlberg's house just after two p.m. Jason had known Dwayne for several years. Confined to a wheelchair, he was somewhat limited in where he could venture during the day, since not many of their friends had cars large enough to accommodate him and his equipment. A couple of years before, Dwayne had driven his car off a cliff on a drunken dare from friends, and the collision had broken his back and rendered him paralyzed from the waist down.

Three female friends came over, and they all drove to Gates Canyon Park to smoke marijuana together. The crew dropped Jason at his friend Jason Stout's house, just down the street from Dahlberg's, at around three forty-five. Stout was in his room asleep, but Jason roused him while the others drove to Taco Bell to fetch food. They returned about a half hour later. They played Ping-Pong for a bit and drank gin from Stout's father's liquor cabinet mixed with Sunny Delight. Jason Stout then pulled out a bottle of Southern Comfort, from which Jason Holland took several shots. He drank a second gin and Sunny D. So, between three forty-five and six thirty p.m., Jason had consumed a minimum of four hard alcohol drinks.

Chris Velardo pulled up in his truck with Micah, Brandon, and Tony around six thirty, and they had to clear out quickly because Stout's father was due home any minute and would have been beyond angry to find that they had partied that afternoon at his house. The five boys drove to Gates Canyon Park just before seven p.m. to continue drinking. Velardo's plan was to drop the boys at the park, then head back to pick up Dwayne Dahlberg and his wheelchair, so he could continue partying as well. But instead, Jason jumped out of the truck, immediately opened the door to Alyce Moulder's van, and snatched her wallet off the dashboard. "I just took it," he said. Then he shouted, "Let's go!" to Chris. He wanted to get out of there quickly, before Ms. Moulder saw them.

Jason admitted to tossing the wallet from the truck just as

they pulled out of the parking lot after noticing that there was nothing of value in it. When asked about Alyce Moulder's story, and the confrontation in the strip mall parking lot, Jason said that none of that actually happened the way Ms. Moulder had recalled. Yes, they had driven to a pizza place near Village Market, the small liquor store on Las Virgenes Road. Alyce Moulder found them there, shouted at them, and they all shouted back. She had tried to hit them with her car, and then she immediately sped off. None of them had thrown rocks at her car; nor did Chris Velardo own a Club locking device that Jason knew of. He insisted many times that he had never seen a Club device inside Chris Velardo's truck.

Jason and Brandon were lying in the bed of the truck while they drove out of the Village Market parking lot and hopped onto the 101 freeway. Chris, Tony, and Micah sat up front. When the truck stopped, Jason and Brandon had no idea where they were. Micah and Tony exited the truck, then hopped over the McLoren fence. Chris Velardo explained that they were swinging by McLoren's fort to "buy some weed." Jason thought that sounded good. He jumped out of the truck bed, followed the others, and climbed over the fence.

Jason said he and Brandon followed Micah and Tony, who were roughly twenty feet or so in front of them. Jason was fairly inebriated by this time, so he explained that he was walking sluggishly. He saw Mike and Jimmy working out and punching the bag. As Micah approached, McLoren said, "What's up, Micah?" Mike and Micah walked into the fort together. By the time Jason approached, he said the two had started fighting. "My brother was down, and Mike was already on top of him." It was very dark inside the fort, and as he reached out to grab Mike's wrist, Jason was punched in the face and fell to the floor facedown. As Jason pushed himself up with his hands, Mike—who still had Micah in a headlock—kicked him right in the face. As Jason struggled to stand, he saw McLoren on top of Micah, still pummeling him in the back of the neck and head. "I was scared for my brother," he said.

Unable to pull Mike from Micah, Jason made a spontaneous and drunken decision. A life-altering one. He reached into a pouch on his waist, pulled open his pocketknife, and "pricked him in the back." Mike McLoren continued pounding away. "I didn't want to hurt him. I just wanted to scare him off my brother. And I was still yelling for him to get off of him. And he wouldn't get off him." He pricked him a second time.

Jason was then "grabbed from behind" and spun around. "I was just kind of freaking out in there. I was scared. It all happened so fast." He knew then that he had pushed the knife into Jimmy. Still, it seemed pretty unbelievable that a small blade could do much damage. Mike and Jimmy both jumped up and ran toward the McLoren house. Jason, Micah, Tony, and Brandon walked back toward the truck. Once inside the truck bed, Jason looked at the knife and saw "just a thin line of red near the handle."

Imagine all the tiny, seemingly unimportant split-second decisions that were made that day. Originally Chris had planned to drop the crew off so they could party at McLoren's for a bit, then return to retrieve Dwayne Dahlberg with his wheelchair and bring him over. Imagine if Jason Holland and Brandon Hein had remained lying on their backs in the truck bed, too relaxed and happy to get up. Would Jimmy Farris still be alive? If Chris Velardo hadn't lingered as long as he did, and instead returned immediately to pick up Dwayne as planned, he probably would never have been charged with anything.

Jason described heading back to Jason Stout's house for the night, calling his mother from the phone in his friend's bedroom, and learning that Jimmy Farris had died. Once he looked out the front window and saw the approaching car headlights—of what looked to be a police car—he fled out the back door. He said he'd decided to "hide for a while," although he refused to name anybody who had helped him, or say where exactly he went. He did describe wandering around Southern California, and said he mostly just hid out wherever he could. Once he saw his name and face on television, then learned that he and Brandon could face the death penalty, and Micah, Tony, and Chris had been charged with murder, he returned home. Jason surrendered, and immediately told authorities that he was to blame. None of the other boys had weapons. Nobody knew he had a knife, nor that he had stabbed anybody, he insisted. Jason took full responsibility for the death of Jimmy Farris. And he was clear in stating that it would have been unfair to punish the others for his grave mistake.

Jason concluded on an emotional note. "There was a fight. It was an accident. I didn't mean for that to happen."

TURNING POINT

PROSECUTOR JEFFREY SEMOW APPROACHED JASON
at the witness stand. He stood close and immediately referred
to him as a "sociopath," who was honoring a "gang code," even
though Judge Mira had previously ruled that any discussion of
gangs was inadmissible. Semow was on fire with his interrogation of Jason. Quick, articulate, and full of passion, the prosecutor laid the foundation for the boys enjoying a "crime spree"
throughout the day, beginning with the taking of liquor from
Jason Stout's house.

"What were you drinking?"

"Gin mixed with Sunny Delight."

"The gin came from his father's liquor cabinet?"

"I guess."

"You didn't see where he got it?"

"No."

"You knew that this was his father's liquor."

"Yeah."

"You knew that his father didn't want you to take it."

"Jason [Stout] just said we could drink it, I guess."

"You knew that his father didn't want you to take it."

"I figured . . ."

"So you knew you were *stealing* it, didn't you?"

"I guess."

"You weren't borrowing it, were you?"

"No."

"You knew if he had seen you do it, he would say, 'Heck, no!' Didn't you?"

"Yes."

"But you did it anyway."

"We just wanted to drink."

"Well, is there something in particular about the taste of gin?"

"No. We just . . . I don't know. We just . . . something to do, I guess."

Semow then described how Chris, Brandon, Micah, and Tony later showed up, and they grabbed the bottle of Southern Comfort to continue drinking at Gates Canyon Park. "Everybody knew that Jason Stout hadn't gone out on his own and bought a bottle of Southern Comfort, didn't they?" He continued. "Anybody say to you, 'Hey—we shouldn't be drinking?' I'm talking about your codefendants in this case and also Chris Velardo. Did anybody say, 'Hey, we shouldn't be doing this? This alcohol does not belong to us'?" The answer was, "No." Of course they hadn't.

Jeffrey Semow wasted no time in hammering right into the issue of credibility, which was the crux of the entire case.

"Mr. Holland, you understand that the credibility of every single witness in this case is an issue, don't you?"

"Yes."

"You understand that what we mean when we talk about credibility of a witness is his honesty or dishonesty?"

"Yes."

"You judge a person's honesty by his actions, don't you?"

"Yes."

"Judging yourself from your actions on May 22, 1995, are you an honest person?"

(PAUSE)

"Are you an honest person, Mr. Holland?"

"I made some mistakes."

"Mr. Holland, did you hear my question?"

"I am an honest person."

"Were you an honest person when you opened the door to Miss Moulder's car?"

"No."

"Were you an honest person when you took Jason Stout's father's booze?"

"No."

"When you reached into Miss Moulder's car, and took her wallet, were you being honest?"

"No."

"When you slammed the door of her car shut and jumped into

the bed of the truck, were you being an honest person?"

"No."

"When you told Chris Velardo, 'Let's get out of here!' were you being an honest person?"

"No."

"When you were driving down the road, looking through the wallet, what were you looking for?"

"Money."

"Because if there was any money, you were going to take it, weren't you?"

"Most likely."

"Would an honest person do that, Mr. Holland?"

Mr. Semow continued firing uncomfortable questions. He slowly moved closer and closer toward Jason as he proceeded. At several points, Attorney Ira Salzman was forced to object and ask the judge to reprimand Mr. Semow. "He's only inches from his face!"

"How many times had you been in Chris Velardo's car before?"

"I can't count."

"Too many to count?"

"Just, I never took a note or anything."

"Had you always sat in the bed of the truck?"

"No."

"You've sat up in the cab before?"

"Yeah."

"You see those pictures of the car, don't you, up on the big board?"

There were several evidence exhibits, including giant photographs. One was of the interior of Chris Velardo's truck.

"I want you to look at the people's exhibit 6F, Mr. Holland, and tell us what it is you see on the steering wheel."

"A . . . Club."

Semow moved immediately into questions about Jason's knife. Specifically, he aimed to prove that Jason carried a pocketknife with a lock-back for a specific reason. On certain pocketknives, a lock-back feature enables the spine to lock into a notch on the back of the blade when it is opened. The blade stays locked open so that it won't slip closed and accidentally cut fingers. When he had gone to Big 5 Sporting Goods to purchase a knife, Semow wondered, why hadn't he chosen a regular Swiss Army knife? After all, a knife of that brand contained a toothpick, a corkscrew, and different-size blades. The Gerber knife he chose had none of those things.

"What do you do with your knife, Mr. Holland?"

"I don't know."

"Do you carve wood?"

"No."

"Did you have some kind of a job that you used a knife for?"

"No."

"Did you have some kind of occupation or craft that you were engaged in that you had the use of a knife?"

"No."

"Well, then . . ."

"I don't know. Always liked pocketknives, I guess."

"Just liked knives? Was there any reason why you got a lock-back knife instead of a regular pocketknife?"

"No."

"And you know, don't you, Mr. Holland, that the big difference is you can't use a Swiss Army knife in a fight. But you can use a lock-back. You know that, don't you?"

"I . . . I guess you could use a Swiss Army knife."

"Isn't that, Mr. Holland, because a lock-back is a good fighting knife and a knife without a lock is no good for fighting?"

"Never entered my mind."

It was time to go in for the kill. There was no evidence that any of the boys were members of the Gumbys, and it had been proven that the Gumbys group was not a real gang anyway. Still, Semow had a plan. He looked Jason in the eye and raised his voice.

Prosecutor Semow: Do you know what Gumbys is?

Mr. Leftwich: Objection, Your Honor!

Mr. Salzman: Objection!

Judge: Sustained.

Sustained in legalese means that the question was inappropriate, and the defendant is, therefore, told not to answer. A jury should act as if they'd never heard it.

Jeffrey Semow paused, looked at the jury, then turned back to Jason Holland.

Prosecutor Semow: You know what Gumbys is?

Mr. Salzman: Your Honor, objection!

Judge: Sustained!

Prosecutor Semow: ARE YOU A MEMBER OF THE GUMBYS?

Mr. Salzman: Objection!

Jill Lansing: Objection!

Mr. Leftwich: Oh my God.

Judge: Sustained, Mr. Semow!

Judge Mira had clearly told the lawyers in this case that any mention of gangs was inadmissible, and certainly unethical. Still, part of the prosecution's plan was to hammer away at the gang theory. After all, if a jury hears something enough times, it doesn't matter if a judge instructs them to disregard it. They cannot "unhear" what they've heard.

All four defense attorneys called for a mistrial. Jeffrey Semow had clearly broken the rules with respect to the prejudicial effect of his words. But inflaming the jury was a risk Semow was willing to take. He knew the chance of Judge Mira ordering a mistrial, and therefore starting all over again from scratch after several weeks, was extremely slim. Semow earned a "citation of misconduct" from the judge, which basically amounted to less than a slap on the wrist, and then Mira ordered that the trial would continue.

CLOSING

ANOTHER WEEK WENT BY BEFORE THE DEFENSE AND prosecution decided to wrap up their cases with closing arguments. For three days attorneys for both sides summarized the facts. Jeffrey Semow and Michael Latin insisted that Mike McLoren was "a very credible and powerful witness." They compared Jason, Micah, Brandon, and Tony to a "pack of wolves preying on bunny rabbits." Michael Latin added phrases like, "They are not nice people, are they? They are not good people, are they?" At one point, he implied that there were probably two or three knives involved in the attack, and that Jason Holland was covering for the others. He was dishonest about everything else, Latin concluded, why not this? He pointed to the coroner's autopsy report, which had described two knife wounds found on Jimmy Farris's torso. He explained that the angles of the two puncture wounds suggested knives approaching from different directions, thus indicating there may have been two stabbers. However, he failed to mention that, according to all the testimony, this was a very physical fight with all five boys inside the fort twisting and turning and rolling in various directions. The single knife could have easily come at Jimmy from two different angles at two different times.

Micah Holland's attorney, James Sussman, said, "These are kids going to, unfortunately, a drug dealer's residence, and all hell breaks loose." The defense painted the event as a drug deal gone bad, which resulted in an accidental death. None of the defendants could have possibly seen it coming.

Jill Lansing reminded the jury that—by law—they could find the defendants guilty only if they believed the other boys aided and abetted (meaning they planned the stabbings), or if there was no doubt that all four boys drove to McLoren's house to burglarize the fort. Jill Lansing also implied that perhaps Mike McLoren had changed his initial story only after the police discovered he was a drug dealer. Her theory was that Mike invented a story about the boys trying to rob him in exchange for protection from prosecution for selling marijuana. If he could help the prosecution to secure a conviction based on him insisting he was being robbed, perhaps they would then fail to charge him for selling drugs. Lansing ended her arguments by reiterating that the entire case for the prosecution was based on stories told by a proven liar.

The trial wrapped up on Friday, May 10, 1996. However, one juror had a previously scheduled vacation for the following week, so the jury could not convene for deliberations until Monday, May 20. The Memorial Day weekend was also coming up, so it wasn't until Tuesday, May 28, 1996—one year and six days after Jimmy Farris's death—that all six families involved would finally gain some form of closure.

VERDICT

SEVEN WOMEN AND FIVE MEN WERE LED INTO THE
courtroom on that Tuesday morning. They took their seats in the
jury box. Judge Mira announced that he was instructing the defendants, their families, and spectators to hold any reactions or words
until all verdicts were read and he had adjourned court. Nobody
was allowed to express any emotions until they were outside the
courtroom. Easy for Judge Mira. Not so easy for anybody else. Jeffrey Semow looked behind him to the Farris family, where Judie
and Jim were clutching each other tightly. He later said, "Judie was
literally holding her breath." Jason, Micah, Brandon, and Tony, all
dressed in long-sleeved shirts and ties, stood silent and still.

The jury foreman stood. On the charges of the attempted
murder of Mike McLoren:

*We, the jury, find the defendants Jason Holland, Micah Holland,
Brandon Hein, and Tony Miliotti . . .*

. . . not guilty.

On the charges of first-degree murder of Jimmy Farris with special circumstances:

We, the jury, find the defendants Jason Holland, Micah Holland, Brandon Hein, and Tony Miliotti . . .

. . . guilty.

SHOCK

SHARRY HOLLAND SAT IN THE FRONT ROW OF THE courtroom, her face and neck washed with tears, unable to rise to her feet. She shook her head back and forth while she watched as her two sons were led away by bailiffs. Gene Hein walked outside, then doubled over a railing and sobbed. Sharry Holland finally walked out of the courthouse, then sat motionless on a bench with her head down. Neither of the parents spoke to the press. They were physically unable to speak.

Mike Miliotti, Tony Miliotti's uncle, told reporters, "It makes no sense. The guy who did it admitted to it in court and admitted no one else had anything to do with it." Micah Holland's attorney, James Sussman, added, "In twenty years as an attorney, I've never experienced such a miscarriage of justice."

Jason's attorney, Ira Salzman, expressed complete shock at the conviction of first-degree murder with special circumstances.

"Jason was presented, and fairly so, of having been guilty of unreasonable use of force. Which sadly took a life. But whatever he did was motivated by concern for his brother." Salzman had fully expected Jason to be found guilty of voluntary or involuntary manslaughter. "And," he added, "I believed the other three would have been acquitted." Salzman went on to explain that because of the peaceful suburban setting of Agoura Hills, and therefore the unprecedented media coverage, prosecutors Jeffrey Semow and Michael Latin used the events to make it "some major moral crusade." He added that if this exact scenario had occurred in the gang-infested neighborhoods of South Central Los Angeles or Compton, the verdicts would have been more "fair and just." Salzman felt that sending any of these boys to prison for life would be a completely improper use of the system's harshest punishment, next to the death penalty. "We want to reserve one of the more onerous punishments we have for cold-blooded intentional murderers. Even the prosecutors can't say with a straight face that there was intent to kill here!"

Jeff Ladin, Tony's other uncle, who had raised him from childhood and attended every single hearing and trial date, discussed the gang angle with reporters. "The lawyers objected," he said, "but the damage was done. You could see it in the jurors' faces." Just after this discussion, the families watched while groups of police officers provided each juror with private escorts as they returned to their cars. The defense attorneys were shocked. In all their years of working criminal cases, many of which were gang related, none had ever seen a jury demand police escorts. The prosecution had succeeded in frightening the jurors, so much so that they felt compelled to put these "gang members" behind bars. Prior to revealing the verdict, jury members had met with Judge Mira in his chambers and requested unprecedented police protection. Their fear, they claimed, was that their lives were in danger. They wanted to prevent retaliation from these people, this gang, called the Gumbys.

Sentencing was set for July 15, 1996. Judge Mira had ultimate control over the futures of all four boys. He would take another six weeks to decide what those fates would be.

JUROR NUMBER 10

ON JULY 15, 1996, ALL FIVE FAMILIES ONCE AGAIN FILED into the Malibu Municipal Courthouse. Even though all four boys had been found guilty, their sentences were completely up in the air. Nobody involved in the case had any clue which way Judge Mira was leaning. There was an enormous range of possible outcomes. Mira could have enforced the maximum sentence of life in prison, or ordered a few years of detention with probation, or anything in between. The Hein, Holland, and Miliotti clans clutched papers with jotted notes so they could beg for leniency from Judge Mira when allowed to speak. Judie and Jim Farris had prepared speeches of their own. The atmosphere was tense, somber.

But as the sentencing got under way, the four defense attorneys approached the bench. They urged Judge Mira to give them more time to prepare. Some new information had surfaced in the last couple of weeks. Specifically, Jill Lansing pointed to a letter that had been sent to Judge Mira and the other attorneys one day after the May 28 verdict. Per California law, jurors enjoyed full anonymity, so that nobody could ever contact them after a trial. But Juror Number Ten came out of the shadows to express her dire concern. What she described in her letter could have amounted to juror misconduct and grounds for a new trial.

Jill Lansing read the letter out loud to the packed courtroom. Juror Number Ten explained how she had not fully understood the jury instructions. She never felt like there was proper evidence to convict the four boys of first-degree murder. Still, after several days of deliberations, she felt pressured to vote with the majority. In a California murder trial, a jury must acquit or convict with a unanimous vote. Even one outlier who refuses to vote with the rest can result in a "hung jury." This basically amounts to negating the trial, as if it never happened. Prosecutors and defense attorneys must begin all over from square one with a new jury. Prosecutors especially loathe hung juries. Dismissing a trial as if it never occurred can appear to be a waste of taxpayers' money, and certainly a waste of time, energy, and effort for dozens of people involved in the trial. The problem for jurors is that they are human. Most have jobs and families and lives they must return to. After a nine-week trial, and several days of deliberations, this jury group undoubtedly grew weak and tired and really just wanted it to be over. That's when those on the opposite side of the majority, or those on the fence, tend to cave to peer pressure. Nobody wants to feel like his or her life was interrupted for several months for no reason at all, and with no closure.

Further, Juror Number Ten described a scene she witnessed just after the verdict was read that upset and concerned her. After Defense Attorney Ira Salzman and Prosecutors Jeffrey Semow and Michael Latin met and spoke briefly with the jury, which they are allowed to do if the jury complies, Mike McLoren entered the room with Jim and Judie Farris. The others watched as one of the jurors jumped up and embraced McLoren and the Farris family. Somebody on that jury actually knew the victim's family and the state's star witness.

When called to jury duty and questioned before serving on a trial, potential jurors are interrogated thoroughly by defense and prosecuting attorneys. One of the first things they are asked is if they are acquainted with anybody involved in the trial on either side. Jurors have an ethical obligation to disclose any such connections. If they answer yes, they are excused, so they can't impose bias. Nobody will ever know what exactly went down in that jury deliberation room. Again, jurors enjoy total anonymity for life. And they have no obligation to speak of the case again once it is over. There may have been a ringleader, or possibly more than one, who persuaded others to convict. What if one of those ringleaders just happened to have secret personal relationships with the Farris family and Mike McLoren?

During the nine weeks of the trial, there had been rumors swirling around that somebody on the jury knew the victims and their families. Now there was proof. But Judge Mira said he had no interest in what happened after the verdict. And he certainly did not seem to care one bit if the jury was unethically swayed. Mira rejected the defense requests to probe into jury misconduct. He had difficulty concealing his anger at the defense attorneys. "I am not at all pleased that experienced lawyers of the caliber we have here were not able to put together motions in six weeks." He did, however, agree to delay sentencing until August 19. Then he added, "I do not intend to continue this case again." Another full month would pass before Jason, Micah, Brandon, and Tony would have any idea what their futures held.

Prosecutors Jeffrey Semow and Michael Latin strongly opposed the delay. "They are trying to delay the inevitable," Latin said. "We think that is a shame. The victim's family deserves their day in court. They are emotionally prepared for the sentencing. It will be devastating for them to have to wait again."

"It was a bit of a letdown," Judie Farris added. "I hope it won't happen again."

OPINIONS

THOUGH WAITING ANOTHER MONTH WOULD BE brutal for absolutely everybody involved, at this point more time could only help Jason, Micah, Brandon, and Tony. Experts and those who knew the boys best would now have more time to craft opinions and write letters in support of lighter sentences. Judge Lawrence Mira had a monumental decision to make. Delivering the sentences in this highly publicized trial would become one of the most controversial rulings of his career. The lives of four teenage boys now hung on this one man's opinion alone.

But it seemed the whole world had opinions on what sentences Jason, Micah, Brandon, and Tony should face. Letters had been pouring into Judge Mira's office since the verdict was read on May 28. The two letters that stood out the most were from completely opposite sides.

July 18, 1996

Honorable Judge Lawrence J. Mira
Malibu Superior Court
23525 West Civic Center Way
Malibu, California 90265

Dear Judge Mira,

I have a tangential but personal connection with the Farris case. I was the emergency physician at Westlake Hospital who struggled to save Jimmy Farris' life. He died, despite my best efforts, and the efforts of a surgeon and emergency personnel. I also had the sad task of informing his parents of his death.

As the further tragedy of this case unfolded, I can't help but wonder how the outcome could have been different. Life and death in a case of trauma is often a case of moments and millimeters. Jimmy Farris did not die of grossly brutal wounds. Only a single small puncture wound penetrated his chest and into his heart. Had that stab wound been one inch further to the left, he perhaps would still be alive today—and just as important, four other young men would not be on the verge of losing their life's potential. The irony is, that as an emergency physician, I have seen many, many victims, far more heinously injured than the late Jimmy Farris, who nevertheless survive, and whose assailants are punished little.

Fate has indeed dealt Jimmy Farris and his four young attackers a cruel blow.

Although I have no knowledge of the true character of the convicted defendants, I feel that it would be a grave injustice if all these young men—certainly those that did not wield the knife—were given life sentences.

I commiserate with the loss and grief of the Farris family. But there is an old adage, "two wrongs don't make a right." This crime was wrong but a "life sentence" would be wrong too for four young boys who, though guilty, are victims as well—victims of our political times and of unfortunate circumstance.

As you exercise your duty to serve justice, I hope you will also remember that you have the gift of mercy.

Sincerely and respectfully,
Barry Pollack, M.D.

June 27, 1996

The Honorable Lawrence Mira
Judge of the Municipal Court
23525 Civic Center Way

Dear Judge Mira:
I would like to express my thoughts concerning the

four defendants who were recently found guilty of first degree murder with special circumstances for the senseless killing of 16 year old Jimmy Farris. It is my understanding that you will sentence these four defendants on July 15, 1996.

After reviewing the circumstances in this case, I do not believe that these defendants deserve any leniency from the law. Jimmy Farris was brutally stabbed in the heart and his close friend whom he died protecting, might also have died from stab wounds had it not been for prompt medical care.

I understand that a defendant's age at the time of the crime is a factor to be considered in determining whether a minor should be sentenced to life in prison without possibility of parole, or receive a lesser sentence of 25 years to life. With this in mind, I would like to focus my attention upon defendants Micah Holland and Tony Miliotti, who were both minors at the time the crime was committed.

Every decent person who knew Jimmy Farris regarded him as a fine young man. He died a hero, trying to protect his friend from being savagely beaten by four hoodlums. This belief was shared by the jury of 12 people who found all four defendants guilty of murder in the first degree with special circumstances.

The defendants in this case deserve the same mercy they showed to Jimmy Farris and his friend Michael

McLoren. I urge you to sentence all of these defendants to the maximum punishment of life in prison without the possibility of parole. Anything less would be a grave injustice to the fine young man they brutally murdered, to his family, and to his friends and his neighbors.

I thank you for your time and your consideration in the matter.

Very truly yours,
Willie L. Williams
Chief of Police

Why would LAPD Chief of Police Willie Williams feel the need to weigh in on this case, which he had nothing to do with and which was outside his jurisdiction? As soon as this letter was published in the newspapers, rumors swirled around suggesting that Jim Farris Senior, because he was a veteran police officer with the LAPD, had come down heavy on this case and spent a lot of time and political energy influencing the strategy and outcome.

NOT SO HONORABLE?

JUST AFTER ELEVEN O'CLOCK ON A HOT SUMMER night back in July 1992, police officers were called to the scene of a one-car accident on Cornell Road in Agoura Hills. The victim had crashed his yellow Nissan 300ZX sports car into a dirt embankment. Although he appeared uninjured, he was acting loopy, so the officers gave him a sobriety test. He failed miserably. He was lucky to have avoided killing himself or anybody else. The perpetrator "was very cooperative" with police and agreed to a blood alcohol test. It measured 0.14, nearly two times the legal limit. He was immediately arrested for drunk driving. But his case presented a unique and bizarre jurisdictional problem, because it occurred within the territory covered by the court of one Judge Lawrence Mira.

The problem? The culprit *was* Judge Lawrence Mira.

Forty-nine-year-old Judge Lawrence Mira went right back

to work on the Friday after his 1992 arrest. He pleaded guilty to drunk driving one week later. "I'm guilty," he said during his hearing. "I plead guilty, and I expect to be punished as any other citizen." But it's not clear that he was punished like any other citizen. The judge paid $901 in fines and was forbidden to drive for the next three months, except to and from work. No jail time. No losing his license. No community service hours picking up trash at city parks while wearing a fluorescent orange vest. His reprimand amounted to a slight slap on the wrist compared to what many first-time offenders charged with driving under the influence would have received in California in 1992. Maximum penalties included six months of jail time, thousands of dollars in fines, and lengthy probation.

Those in the district attorney's office applauded "Larry's" handling of his arrest and hearing. "Everybody makes mistakes," was the phrase heard most often from prosecutors. Judge Mira had worked with the Los Angeles district attorney's office as a prosecutor prior to Governor Deukmejian appointing him to a judge position just five years before. The fact that he owned up to breaking the law really "shows good character," one deputy DA said. Wouldn't a man of good character, whose life's work it was to protect and enforce the law, have avoided driving drunk in the first place? How hard was it to ride with somebody else or call a cab? Wasn't that what they always taught high school students? *If you are impaired, don't get behind the wheel. Get a ride.*

Another former coworker described Judge Mira as "a living-on-the-edge sort of guy." Still, he added, "he's politically skilled."

Another Los Angeles Municipal judge, Edward L. Davenport, had been battling drunk driving charges all year long using a very different approach. After his arrest he had refused to submit a blood alcohol test. He had already gone through two criminal trials, both resulting in mistrials, and was about to embark on a third. Judge Mira was praised for admitting to his mistake and accepting consequences. Not to mention saving taxpayer money by pleading guilty and avoiding a trial.

Just the year before, the California Commission on Judicial Performance, an ethical oversight agency that evaluated judges, reprimanded another judge after a DUI conviction and stated, "The judge failed to observe the high standard of conduct expected of California judges and has diminished public confidence in the judiciary." Had Judge Mira's behavior diminished public confidence in the judiciary? It didn't much matter. No judge in California history has ever been removed from office for a drunk driving conviction.

THE NEW NORMAL

THE PARADOX OF RELIEF MIXED WITH ANXIETY THAT the defendants and their families experienced after Judge Mira postponed the sentencing ate away at their sanity. On one hand, the idea that "no news is good news" at least provided some optimism that the judge could still show mercy on the teens. They were given the gift of six more weeks of hope. On the other hand, waking up every day to the complete unknown about the future was maddening.

When asked what she'd say to Judge Mira if she could just sit down and talk with him, Sharry Holland answered, "I'd ask him to search his heart. I don't see how anybody could think that prison for any of them is fair. How can they just throw the boys' lives away over a mistake, an accident, an unplanned, chaotic backyard fight?" Judge Mira knew all about stupid mistakes, didn't he?

Visiting hours for both the LA County Men's Central Jail and Central Juvenile Hall were held on weekends. Awake and out of the house before the crack of dawn every Saturday and Sunday, Sharry faithfully visited Jason and Micah at the two facilities. Jason was held in isolation because the crime was considered one of "celebrity status." Because the trial had garnered so much attention and press, Jason remained in solitary confinement for what Los Angeles County called "his own protection." Only a fraction of those inmates held in solitary confinement were allowed visits with family on any given day, so it was up to Sharry be first in line on weekends. Visiting hours at Men's Central Jail began at ten a.m., and most visitors were turned away.

Sharry immediately noticed that soon after being put into isolation, Jason stopped looking her in the eyes during visits. "He doesn't even realize he isn't looking at me," she said. Visits with Jason were noncontact, so he and his mother could only speak via corded phone and through thick Plexiglas. Visits were limited to twenty minutes, maximum. All conversations were recorded. Guards hovered and watched every tiny movement, heard every single word. Mother and son were not allowed to touch anymore, so they pressed their hands up to the glass while they spoke. The only personal items Jason was allowed to possess in his cell were paperback books. Sharry mailed as many as she could, because visitors were not allowed to bring any gifts into the jail. He loved reading, particularly mysteries and Westerns. Because Jason was a legal adult, there was no law dictating that he attend school or enjoy daily recreation. His life was reduced to reading, eating, and sleeping. That was it.

For Sharry, it was nice to see Micah in a more relaxed environment than the Men's Central Jail offered. They were allowed to hug once as she arrived, and they sat across from each other at stainless-steel dayroom tables with no Plexiglas separating them.

When talking with Jason and Micah, either by phone once a week or during visits, conversations were often strained and awkward. "Sometimes I can't figure out what in the world to say," Sharry admitted. "I'll ask, 'What are you doing?' But what do I think they are doing? There isn't much to do in there!"

Sharry explained to reporters that Jason simply could not stomach the idea that Micah, Brandon, and Tony could actually be punished as severely as he might be. "He thinks it's pretty much, 'I know my life is over.' But it shouldn't be for the other boys." On many occasions Jason said that he would willingly put in any amount of hard prison time—life, if necessary—if Judge Mira would just let the others go.

FISSURES

ON THE MORNING OF SATURDAY, AUGUST 3, 1996, the *Los Angeles Times* ran an article announcing that Jim and Judie Farris had filed a wrongful death civil suit, claiming pecuniary loss and seeking punitive damages. They had filed about two months previously, the day before the statute of limitations to file such a suit ran out. Pecuniary loss generally refers to income lost because of the death. Usually, these are filed when a parent or breadwinner has perished, and the family needs help financially. Punitive damages aim to punish the wrongdoers because they either had malicious intent, or exhibited negligence that allowed the death to occur. Those named in the civil suit were Jason and Micah Holland, Brandon Hein, Tony Miliotti, Chris Velardo, Sharry Holland, and Gene Hein. It came as a shock to all involved when an additional four names were added to the suit. The Farris family was also suing Mike McLoren, Nancy McLoren, and her parents.

The defendants, their families, and their attorneys were all surprised at the sudden rift between the Farris and McLoren families. The suit claimed that Nancy McLoren and her parents were negligent in keeping abreast of what Mike was up to out in his backyard fort and, therefore, were responsible for Jimmy's death. It seemed strange, because Mike McLoren had appeared so tight with the Farris family during the trial. Brandon's attorney, Jill Lansing, said, "Why would the Farris family want to punish Mike McLoren and his schoolteacher mother and his grandparents? I'm sure they are very hurt by this."

Both Jill Lansing and Jim Sussman suggested that the reason the prosecution was so adamant about getting the sentencing out of the way immediately was so that news about the civil suit would not come out until afterward. Now that the cat was out of the bag, the implication was that perhaps Mike McLoren was more culpable than anyone had previously thought. Still, the Farris family had desperately needed Mike McLoren and his testimony during the trial, as it was the only evidence that could convict the Holland brothers, Brandon, and Tony. The most upsetting part of this whole twist in the story was that Gene Hein and Sharry Holland were not wealthy people. They had spent most of their savings paying for expensive attorneys during the last year or so. Not to mention that they had lost significant wages after taking time off work to attend court hearings and the nine-week trial. And, now, a civil wrongful death suit meant they would probably lose everything they owned, including their homes.

Jill Lansing continued. "They are deeply hurt by the loss of a child. But short of having a child die, I can't think of anything harder than looking at your eighteen-year-old son and knowing that he is going to die in prison. And to have your house taken away on top of that seems to be vindictive."

Sharry Holland had difficulty hiding her displeasure. "I only have three things. I have my daughter, a lot of bills, and a leased car. And the only one of those things they can have are the bills."

LAST CHANCE FOR MERCY

DEFENSE ATTORNEYS CAME IN WITH GUNS BLAZING on Monday, August 19. They had been granted an additional four weeks to prepare their arguments in favor of mercy for the boys. Their ammunition was a long list of motions they wanted Judge Mira to consider before handing down the final sentences. Once the sentences were set, that was the point of no return. The defense attorneys filed motions asking for new trials. Denied. They submitted a motion to obtain contact information for the jurors so they could investigate juror misconduct. Denied. Pointing to the pending wrongful death lawsuit against Mike McLoren and his family, the defense attorneys filed motions to investigate the terms of the suit in hopes of finding evidence that Mike was, in fact, somehow at fault for Jimmy's death. Denied.

Ira Salzman pleaded with the judge, "Somebody out there believes that he [Mike McLoren] did something wrong."

Judge Mira wouldn't budge. "I am unmoved by your arguments. My earlier rulings will stand."

Much of Monday featured Jill Lansing explaining how her client, Brandon Hein, should be treated differently from the Holland brothers. In fact, she explained, the jury should have had the opportunity to find Brandon guilty of something other than felony murder with special circumstances. After all, Micah Holland demanded the marijuana, and Jason Holland committed the stabbing. Therefore, those two were the criminals. Brandon, like Tony, was a bystander. Although it was part of Jill Lansing's strategy in support of her client Brandon, this was difficult for both the Hein and Holland families to hear.

Gene Hein took the stand to advocate for his son Brandon. He described a sweet boy from a very tight family, who often had dinner waiting on the stove when Gene returned from long days at work. Although he admitted that Brandon had difficulty keeping up in school, and often turned to alcohol, he never spoke back to his parents or ever exhibited any violence. "He's made mistakes. He's made poor choices." Still, Gene insisted, the violent monster the prosecution painted was simply the opposite of who Brandon was. "In looking back, I wish I would have been tougher. I kick myself for that."

Tony's relatives also described him as a calm, kind boy, who loved taking care of his little cousins. "He's soft," one uncle said. "He wouldn't hurt a fly."

When Sharry Holland took the stand, she had a different approach when describing her sons. She detailed the severe verbal and physical abuse both boys suffered at the hands of their biological father when they were very young, and then their stepfather during the eight years he was in their lives. When the boys grew older, it was Jason who stepped in and fought his stepfather, so he could divert attention away from young Micah. When Micah was being beaten, Jason always intervened. His protection of his younger brother was fierce and unwavering. "Abuse has been such a popular defense for crimes in the 1990s," Sharry said. "I feel very uncomfortable with bringing it up. But the point is, it's the truth. We—Micah, Jason, and I—have nothing to hide."

Ira Salzman reminded the judge that they were not asking him to let Jason and Micah off the hook, or even to reduce their sentences to probation. There's "pressure on judges to not appear soft on crime," Salzman had told reporters. Still, the defense attorneys knew full well that both boys would be given prison time. In fact, Salzman added, "We are asking for a lengthy prison term," rather than a full life sentence without any possibility for parole.

Everybody on the Holland team understood that both Jason and Micah would need to be punished. Even Sharry had said, "If I saw them put away for ten years, fifteen years, that would be terrible. But I would be able to say it was justice. To take his life away, though, to take all their lives, it's not human." When asked about her decision to discuss the abuse the boys had suffered, Sharry said, "I feel very self-conscious about it. But how could I leave that out? I'm fighting, trying to make the court understand how this could have happened." In her testimony, she talked about how the most violent beating Jason suffered was when Gary Holland attacked him and broke bones in his face, including his nose. That was back in May 1995, soon before the boys went to Mike McLoren's fort.

EXPERT TESTIMONY

A YOUNG CHILD WILL TAKE WHAT HE'S LEARNED AT home and project it onto how he perceives the world around him. Micah and Jason Holland were not raised in a safe environment. Two of the earliest people embedded in their lives were supposed to nurture and protect, and instead betrayed them. When a small child is taunted and abused unexpectedly without the punishment ever matching the offense, he begins to view the world as unsafe and unpredictable. Micah put on a tough face. When he was frightened of people, he struck preemptively, showing no fear, in hopes he wouldn't get messed with. He liked acting tough. It made him feel powerful in a world where behind closed doors he felt powerless. When a child is raised in an unpredictable environment like that, never knowing when or how the next beating will come, he can either cower into withdrawn depression, or take control by fighting back. Against the world. Anger is way more powerful than sadness. It feels much better, too.

After the defendants' families advocated for them during the sentencing hearings, two clinical psychologists got on the stand and testified on behalf of the Holland brothers. They explained that both boys were extremely remorseful about what happened to Jimmy Farris, and appropriately emotional when recounting the event during therapy sessions. Neither boy had any sociopathic or antisocial tendencies. Both, however, were described as "emotionally immature." And after psychological testing, they'd found that Micah suffered from such extreme attention deficit disorder, they said it would have been near impossible for him to have planned out this sort of attack. After evaluating Micah and Jason, both psychologists agreed they were completely normal teens who reacted impulsively during a fight, and had never gone over to Mike McLoren's house with malicious intent.

At one point, the prosecution was allowed to cross-examine Dr. Ann Thiel, the clinical psychologist who was treating and advocating for Jason. Jeffrey Semow literally screamed at her, as if she were on trial. After the doctor explained that, in her opinion, Jason had been protecting his brother, Micah, and overreacted with his aggression, but did not intend to severely harm or kill anybody, Semow shouted, "Ma'am, did you just fall off the turnip truck?!" The implication that this doctor was a clueless idiot was not only unprofessional, but one of the nastier quotes from the sentencing phase. With folded arms and a lot of eye rolling, prosecutors Jeffrey Semow and Michael Latin had difficulty hiding their annoyance, calling the whole few days a silly "dog and pony show," and "a legally meaningless exercise."

THE PEOPLE VERSUS DILLON

THIS LAST EFFORT TO PERSUADE JUDGE MIRA TO show some mercy was far from meaningless. After all, the man was human. Just like no one can ever know what sliver of information pushes a jury over the edge to acquit or convict, it's impossible to know what story or emotional plea could strike a chord with a judge. Life in prison for Jason, Micah, Brandon, and Tony was disproportionate to the crime committed, according to their attorneys. They cited a precedent—as attorneys usually do—which was a case from 1983, *People v. Dillon*. The defense attorneys spent two full days on the Dillon motion, stating that because of the outcome in that case, Judge Mira was obligated to uphold and respect the law by showing mercy in his sentencing.

Early in the morning back on October 17, 1978, seventeen-year-old Norman Jay Dillon and seven friends drove out to a small private farm in California's Santa Cruz Mountains with the intent of stealing marijuana plants they had discovered growing there. Dillon had scoped out the farm twice before, and both times was scared off by Dennis Johnson, who guarded the crops and carried a shotgun. Dillon and his crew spent weeks planning the robbery, at one point discussing "holding the guy up," "hitting him over the head with something," or "tying him to a tree." They armed themselves with sticks, knives, wire cutters, a baseball bat, paper bags to hold the plants, masks, rope, and maps of the property. Norman Dillon thought it a good idea to bring his own gun to the burglary. Several of the other boys armed themselves with guns as well. The boys climbed a hill, crossed NO TRESPASSING barricades, and hopped a six-foot wire fence. They separated into pairs. While the eight boys spread out, their attempts to steal the plants were constantly thwarted by guards. For nearly two hours they circled, waiting for the guards to step away.

Eventually, two boys abandoned the plan. Two more were chased and attacked by dogs. Then another boy had so much trouble carrying his shotgun, he accidentally discharged it twice. After hearing the shots, Dennis Johnson investigated the ruckus. He spotted the boys and walked toward them. Norman Dillon pulled out his .22 semiautomatic rifle. He shot Johnson point-blank nine times. Dennis Johnson died in the hospital a couple of days later.

After a jury trial, Norman Dillon was found guilty of first-degree felony murder because the killing had occurred during the commission of an attempted robbery. There was no mystery, no question what the boys had planned that morning. Burglary (entering a private dwelling without permission while intending to commit a crime) and robbery (taking property using the threat of force) were the intent, 100 percent. Norman Dillon was handed a sentence of life in prison. None of the other seven boys were convicted of a homicide, even though they were all armed and had methodically planned out the burglary. And then, on appeal, Dillon's conviction was reduced to second-degree murder. This meant that the killing itself was not premeditated. Still, Dillon had what they called "reckless disregard for human life." In other words, the murder wasn't totally planned out, but at the moment he was killing, he meant to kill. And, because of Norman Dillon's age of seventeen, his sentence of life in prison was deemed cruel and unusual. His sentence was greatly reduced. The felony murder rule was tossed out because of his age and immaturity.

Therefore, the defense attorneys argued, Judge Mira needed to take the Dillon case and decision into consideration. Conclusions to trials like these should always be based on precedent. Not to mention that the situation with the Holland brothers, Brandon, and Tony was nowhere near the sophisticated planning of the crime Norman Dillon and his friends committed. Punish the boys, yes, they urged. But please don't condemn them to die in prison.

JUDGMENT DAY

BEFORE JUDGE MIRA GAVE HIS DECISION, HE ASKED to hear from Jimmy Farris's parents. During the sentencing phase of a murder trial, the victim's family usually reads an impact statement. Judie Farris had never been one to hide her rage. She'd always been an open book regarding her feelings. She shook and choked back tears during her entire reading. "You've damaged me, and all this pain has killed a part of me. I'm sentenced for the rest of my life. Nothing will ever get Jimmy out of his coffin, his pine box. You deserve to be confined forever as we are." Judie Farris described how she had felt "brain dead" during the last fifteen months, and unable to even look into Jimmy's empty room. She spent more than an hour detailing Jimmy's full life and how he showered his family with love and joy. She could not recall a single thing he ever did wrong. In fact, she said the worst thing he ever did in his short life was "get toothpaste on the bathroom mirror." At several points, she couldn't read from her notes because her tears literally blinded her. "The first time I had to use a knife to do something, well, you'll never know what that feels like. I can see the coldness in your eyes and meanness in your heart. Look at Jimmy's picture. Look how warm he is! I'm positive that the three of you don't have a conscience. Well, Tony, I'm not sure about you. Because when you looked at me during the trial, it seemed like you were sorry. But today you haven't looked at me at all." Judie Farris held up a lock of long blond hair secured in a rubber band. "This is all I have left of Jimmy." She sobbed. "In the hospital, I cut it. And I wish I had taken more. . . . *This* is all I have left of him, for the rest of my life."

Jim Farris Senior stood behind his wife, his hand on her waist, during her speech. He was less sad, more angry. "My wife and I will never understand why you had to kill him." Jim Farris dispelled some information he felt was lies about his son. "He wasn't a drug user." He then went on to discuss how Jimmy only had "small amounts of marijuana" found in his system during the autopsy. "My family and the community as a whole want you criminals separated from us and punished. You people need to be removed from society so you are no longer able to intimidate, rob, or even kill again." He concluded his impact statement by saying, "My son is dead and you people killed him. And for that you need to be punished to the full extent of the law."

Finally, it was Judge Lawrence Mira's turn to speak. Fifteen months of unbearable waiting had finally reached its climax. He replayed the story as he saw it. All four defendants began their day on Monday, May 22, 1995, looking to cause mayhem. This culminated in a "crime spree" that began when they "stole alcohol" from Jason Stout's house. Judge Mira said he rejected the defense arguments; psychologist testimony and advocacy and stories of child abuse had no bearing on this case. Even if Jason, Micah, Brandon, and Tony were not part of any organized gang, their actions on that day were just the same as any violent street gang. "I believe that on this tragic day, they formed their own gang. The genesis of this group was in their lifestyle, their aimlessness, their purposelessness. They didn't take their education seriously. They rejected their families' values. They adopted a we-do-whatever-feels-good-to-us attitude. *That* . . . is classic hedonism."

Nearly one hundred people, family and close friends, sat with breath held. Many of them wept uncontrollably. Sharry Holland sat in the front row of the courtroom, clutching her rosary. Jason, Micah, Brandon, and Tony all sat motionless, with eyes wide.

Stating that he found the boys to be "remorseless, arrogant, and dangerous," Judge Mira said they exhibited an "arrogant disregard for life and property." Further, the taking of alcohol from the Stout home, then taking Alyce Moulder's wallet from her car proved that they went to Mike McLoren's with the intention to rob him. Their actions established a pattern of behavior on that Monday afternoon, he said. Judge Lawrence Mira concluded the day by handing down their sentences:

Jason Holland: life without the possibility of parole (plus eight years)

Brandon Hein: life without the possibility of parole (plus four years)

Anthony Miliotti: life without the possibility of parole (plus four years)

Micah Holland: twenty-five years to life (plus four years)

Judge Mira said that he was exercising massive leniency for Micah, because of his age. They might as well have received the death penalty. More than likely, all four boys would die in prison.

CHAOS

THE ATMOSPHERE OUTSIDE THE COURTHOUSE ON that Wednesday afternoon, August 21, quickly morphed from tense to explosive. About half the spectators were friends and family of the four defendants. The other half were supporters of the Farris family. At one point, members of Tony Miliotti's family exchanged words with Farris supporters. It quickly escalated to shoving, and the groups had to be separated two times as full-blown fistfights erupted. The irony was painful, almost laughable. Here a sixteen-year-old boy was dead, and four teenage boys were sentenced to die in prison. Yet the adults in this scenario couldn't contain themselves and mourn in a productive or mature manner.

"Justice was done," Jim Farris told reporters. "As far as closure, it doesn't exist. Closure will come when I'm dead."

"Are we so entrenched and so angry that we can't realize that these are boys?" Sharry Holland shot back when it was her turn at the microphone. "I know in my heart that this is so wrong. I believe that people should not be judged on the worst thing they've done in their life."

Gene Hein and Mike Miliotti remained incredulous. "My son is not a murderer," Gene said. "He didn't have a knife. That judgment is not fair. My position is that I know what's right." Gene Hein vowed, "I'll never give up until this comes out the way it should. I'd love to talk with the judge, the prosecutors, and the jury face-to-face. I just don't believe they could believe in what they did after spending an hour with me."

Miliotti expressed that he felt the Farris family wanted revenge. "So for one life they have to take all four."

Brandi Green and Cara Browne, friends of both the Holland brothers and Brandon, cried as they passed around cigarettes in the parking lot with a large group of teens. One girl remarked that she could not believe Micah was going away to prison when he wasn't even shaving yet. An adult friend of the Farris family shouted angrily at the teens, "There's somebody dead here! Good-bye. Gone!" It seemed nobody could see both sides of the tragedy. Everybody chose one side or the other. It was the beginning of a perpetual rift in the community of Agoura Hills and the neighboring towns. Members of both Team Farris and Team Hein/Holland/Miliotti suffered threats, vandalism of cars and homes, angry letters, and broken friendships in the decades to follow.

Within minutes of the verdict being read, all four defense

attorneys submitted paperwork to get the appeals process under way. Sadly, this process often takes a very long time, and experts were estimating that nothing official would be done for the next four to five years. The boys would have to wait until the beginning of the new millennium to find out if they would ever have the slimmest shot at freedom.

LIFERS IN THE BIG HOUSE

LESS THAN TWO MONTHS LATER, ON OCTOBER 7, 1996, Jason and Brandon were strapped into the small white California Department of Corrections van, hands cuffed and legs shackled, heading up Interstate 5 toward the North Kern State Prison Reception Center. The term "reception" generally connotes a warm welcome—in this case, they'd soon find out, it was a misnomer. One hundred eighty miles north of Los Angeles, the NKSP in Delano, California, would be home to the boys for the next couple of months while they were processed, like livestock before slaughter. They didn't talk much during the ride up.

The van departed from LA County Men's Central Jail on the cool, crisp morning, then wove up the 110 freeway. They sped past the business commuters and skyscrapers of downtown Los Angeles, then the Griffith Observatory and its rugged horse and hiking trails, resembling the Valley neighborhoods where they had grown up and roamed free. Once the van merged onto the I-5 freeway, the last scenic view was that of the colorful roller coasters at the famous Six Flags Magic Mountain theme park. Sky-high loops of yellow, blue, and fuchsia tracks hurled screaming guests into the air and upside down as the boys watched, a reminder that their childhoods were officially over. The remainder of the several hours' drive up to Delano featured a whole lot of nothingness. The land grew flatter, browner, and rockier the farther they drove. The only scenery was the occasional dilapidated gas station. The morning had faded into dry afternoon, and the heat rose to ninety-eight degrees by the time they reached the prison.

In the weeks following the sentencing, newspaper reporting on the case petered out. There wasn't much more to say. Gene Hein finally married his longtime girlfriend, Janice. His best-man spot, reserved for Brandon, sat empty during the ceremony. Sharry Holland's daughter, Kylie, celebrated her seventh birthday without her big brothers. Tony Miliotti's father and uncles had difficulty focusing during their long truck driving routes, their minds constantly wandering while worrying about Tony's health and mental state and wondering whether they'd ever see him again.

Once the boys were sentenced to LWOPP in state penitentiaries, visits during the remainder of their time at LA County Men's Jail ceased. Months would pass before Brandon, Jason, or Tony would see their families again. Once they were settled inside a state facility, family members and friends could apply for visits and wait up to six months for state approval. And even then, visits were not guaranteed. There were too many inmates and not enough room to supervise visits, so friends and family members would compete for very few visiting slots.

For the next two to three months, staff at the reception center planned to compile and evaluate Jason's and Brandon's criminal records, life histories, and medical and psychological exams, in order to give them classification scores and determine institutional placement. Now wards of the state, Jason was named K24824, and Brandon K24820. They were numbers now, not humans. The guards at North Kern State Prison welcomed Jason and Brandon with scowls, whispers of "murderer," and promises that they were about to get "messed with" in the worst way possible. "You killed a cop's son," they said. "You are *fucked*. Literally." The staff laughed.

In county jail, they had been lucky. Brandon described it as "pretty easy," compared to what they had envisioned. At least they had enjoyed private cells, a luxury they would rarely see again. Also, in the unit where they had been housed, most inmates were young and just as scared as they had been. Guys in LA County Men's Central Jail were too busy fighting their own cases to bother one another too much. They still had hope for release, for freedom. Prison, however, was a whole different animal.

Now they were entering a whole new world, where beatings, gang politics, and corrupt staff were the norm. Brandon described one officer getting up in his face as he was being processed on the first day. "How you like the view? This look like a nice view to you? You like this? 'Cause this is what you'll be looking at forever." He then pointed toward a new group of inmates who had just received their bedrolls and were walking single file toward them. "You ready for this?" the guard threatened, implying that young, handsome, five-foot-three Brandon was about to be swallowed up and spat out by some of the worst individuals he'd ever meet.

It's no secret that in American society, murdering a police officer is seen as one of the most repugnant crimes imaginable. More than a personal attack, it is viewed as an attack on society and against those who are on the front lines of protecting the public. It is treated as an act of terrorism. As large a state as California is, the world of crime and punishment is remarkably small. Word travels at lightning speed in the prison system. And to be tagged with the murder of a cop's son? That was just about as bad as murdering a cop. There would be no more easy days for Brandon or Jason. The system would guarantee that.

To his delight, however, Brandon realized that out of the twenty or so guys walking past him, he recognized about half of them from County. "What's up, Brandon?" they greeted him. "Good to see you, brother!" Brandon's gift was that he was funny—hilarious, actually—and could talk with absolutely any person from any walk of life. A skilled storyteller, his comedic timing was impeccable, and he could mimic or impersonate just about anybody with the proficiency of a veteran stand-up comic.

His enigmatic ease relaxed people. He had kind, bright-blue eyes and a trustworthy nature that was evident within minutes of meeting him. Warmth radiated from his oversize smile. When he laughed—usually at his own jokes—people couldn't help but laugh with him. A perpetually upbeat kid, his optimism was infectious. These would be his tools for survival.

Brandon and Jason were separated then, led to their new cells, and introduced to their cellies. Brandon described his new roommate as an "older guy," who the guards had warned was ready to fight. But once Brandon took a good look at his cell mate, small but overweight, weak muscle tone, with "man-boobs," he relaxed. He knew he could take the older man if he had to. Fortunately, the guy didn't really have much interest in interacting with him anyway. He ignored Brandon. Bullet dodged.

Although Jason and Brandon were separated, they quickly discovered that they had been placed in cells that shared a vent. Jason was somewhere in a floor above Brandon, and they could communicate through the air vent. Called the prison "telephone," this was a common way for inmates to connect, and it was their lifeline.

In December, Brandon was released from reception and was told he would be transferring to serve his sentence at a brand-new facility, Salinas Valley State Prison, located in Monterey County. The town of Monterey is well-known as one of the most expensive and picturesque seaside towns in the entire country. Brandon remembered traveling on the California Department of Corrections van from the LA County Jail to the Malibu

Courthouse dozens of times in the last year or so. He wondered if this new prison would be situated in an environment similar to the beach town of Malibu. He remembered loving those long drives up the Pacific Coast Highway because it was such a peaceful and refreshing contrast to life in the dark, dungeon-like jail.

But the State of California was strategic in planning their placement of prisons. The criteria for prison building in those planning meetings must have been open land, low population, and the uglier the better. The terrain surrounding the enormous compound was flat, dry, dirty, and rocky, exactly as North Kern had looked. There would be no stunning cliff-side views of the Pacific Ocean or lush vineyards that wove through parts of Monterey County. In fact, there would be no view at all for the next several years, if ever.

"GOOD" NEWS

TWO WEEKS AFTER THE SENTENCING OF THE OTHER
four, Chris Velardo finally had his day in court. Judge Mira was
short and to the point, but not so sweet. Mira explained that he
would allow Chris "time served," which meant that the last sixteen months weren't for nothing. They would count toward his
sentence. Unfortunately for Chris, the speedy trial rule does not
apply to those who have pled guilty to a lesser charge. Therefore,
while the others were waiting, then enduring their trial, Chris
could do nothing but wait in the Sylmar jail until his sentencing.
Per California law, a judge could wait as long as he wanted to.
And Mira certainly took his time. When pleading to voluntary
manslaughter, as Chris had, the maximum sentence allowed in
California was twelve years in state prison. Without explanation,
Judge Mira said, "I sentence you to a term of eleven years in state
prison." Imagine that. Twelve years of a life erased because he

was sitting in a car while an accidental death took place.

But four months later, Chris got some interesting news. Per the terms of his plea agreement, prosecutors Semow and Latin had long before promised him he could serve most of his time in the Youth Authority facilities, not state prison. Anyone sentenced to YA is released on or before his twenty-fifth birthday, by law. But the Youth Authority called the DA's office and said they were rejecting processing of Chris, since the judge had given him a state prison sentence. So the prosecutors had to make a decision. Basically, it was a technical hiccup that could have gone either way for Chris Velardo. Fortunately for him, Semow and Latin kept their word and arranged for him to serve his time at a Youth Authority facility, an environment infinitely safer than adult state prison. Not only that, if luck was on his side and he stayed out of trouble, Chris Velardo could theoretically be released in less than five years. Still not perfect, but much more appealing than putting in eleven years with hardened adult convicts.

BURIED ALIVE

AT THE SAME TIME CHRIS WAS GIVEN THIS NEWS, Jason Holland was strapped into the transport van yet again during a several-hour commute to his new home—Salinas Valley State Prison. He would be joining Brandon. When they found out they were assigned to the same prison, it calmed their nerves. After all, who wants to be sent to a giant house of horrors alone with no familiar faces? What a relief to discover that best friends would be reunited once again. A new Level IV maximum-security prison, SVSP had been quickly rated one of the most violent prisons in California. As the years rolled by, the facility would boast seven hundred to a thousand serious attacks leading to injuries per year. At the time Brandon and Jason arrived in Salinas Valley, though the prison was less than a year old, it was labeled a massive warehouse for California's "worst of the worst," according to one guard. Rehabilitation was not the goal at SVSP. It was literally the place to lock up convicts and throw away the keys.

Jason and Brandon quickly learned that they would both be assigned to a modified SHU. In California, SHU stands for Special Housing Unit, Secure Housing Unit, or Segregated Housing Unit. But it's better known to inmates as "the Box," "the Hole," or "solitary confinement." It was similar to the setup at County, but worse. At Salinas Valley, dozens of windowless eight-by-ten-foot concrete cells opened into one giant concrete hallway. Each steel door featured one vertical sliver of a window so that guards could see in, and a tennis-ball-size cluster of perforated air holes so they could talk to the inmates. One twin-size stainless-steel slab jutted out from the gray cinder-block wall. Two slabs were arranged bunk-bed style for the dual-occupancy cells, which were becoming increasingly common because of overcrowding. Each bed contained one half-inch-thick foam pad, one sheet, and a small papery pillow, like those on examination-room tables in doctors' offices. There was one stainless-steel toilet, with no seat attached, and no privacy door or even a curtain. A small sink sat above the toilet. There were no mirrors. One wall shelf provided storage for a few books, and one dim light hung for reading and writing.

There's a great misconception among many Americans that our prisoners enjoy days filled with gym workout sessions, board games, and television. In reality, an enormous number of our country's inmates spend most of their time in their cells or standing in the yard with not a single ball or piece of equipment. They eat, drink, sleep, and defecate (for those without personal toilets) only when told. Every minute of every day is dictated by the guards.

Inmates are completely stripped of dignity, privacy, and autonomy.

Often compared to being buried alive, SHU offered a special kind of torture. SHU inmates in SVSP were on permanent lockdown twenty-three hours per day. This meant that there would be no communication between prisoners, unless they were assigned a cellie. No television. No music. No gym sessions. No contact at all with the outside world. Three meals per day would be pushed through a horizontal slot in the steel cell door. Inmates were allowed a maximum of ten hours per week of what the state called "recreation." For roughly one hour per day, sometimes a little more, each SHU resident was led outside his cell and placed into—literally—a dog cage, alone. Each dog run consisted of ten square feet of fenced-in dirt. But at least they were outside. A few shallow greenish hills could be seen far off in the distance. On a clear day. If you had twenty-twenty eyesight.

In January 1997 famous journalist Randall Sullivan began research for an article he was writing for *Rolling Stone* magazine about the Agoura Four, as Jason, Brandon, Micah, and Tony were now labeled. He wrote to Jason Holland at Salinas Valley State Prison. Jason wrote back to Sullivan a few days before his twentieth birthday. He explained that being in SHU meant "it's a very serious place to be." He described that he was now locked up with violent career criminals. The thing he most wanted the world to know was that "I'm not some cold-blooded killer. I didn't mean for this to happen and every day I wish I could take it back." Worse than doing time in this hellhole, he said, was the knowledge that

Micah, Brandon, and Tony were paying the ultimate price for a bad decision that he alone had made. "They didn't even see it happen. I took a life and I deserve to be punished. But why take three others that didn't have anything to do with it?"

The use of solitary confinement began in America in the early 1800s but increased exponentially in the 1980s, when strict drug laws and a surge in gang activity caused the US prison population to grow rapidly. Solitary confinement morphed from a last-ditch effort to protect prisoners into an easy way of controlling them. Inmates could get tossed into the hole for minor infractions like raising their voices to a staff member, refusing to eat, hiding food in pockets, or having too many envelopes in their cells. They were at the mercy of the staff, and any one of the guards could have been having a bad day and decided to take it out on an inmate.

The drawbacks of being housed in SHU were endless. Loneliness, boredom, and the torture of having absolutely no contact with any other humans was literally maddening. Being held in solitary confinement has measurable negative physiological effects. The human brain contains a hundred billion cells, with five hundred trillion connections. Brains must interact with the world to survive. It's no surprise then that after enduring just a month or two of solitary, inmates' brains begin to reshape themselves. Connections are lost. Vital portions shrink. The hippocampus connects what we perceive through our senses to the rest of the brain. It is, therefore, crucial to our formation of memories, emotions, and spatial awareness. Damage to the hippocampus can permanently alter a person's depth perception and ability to find their way around even the most familiar of places. Being confined to a small space becomes the norm, and entering larger spaces becomes disorienting and confusing. Hallucinations, severe depression, and emotional outbursts are common. Paranoia sets in rapidly for many. Solitary literally forces serious mental illness on even the most cognitively mature and emotionally healthy people. Its effects on young people under the age of twenty-five had not been studied sufficiently at the time. But there is no doubt its use created severe and lasting brain damage. It would be decades before anybody in the world cared enough to conduct scientifically valid studies on the effects of solitary confinement on young brains.

During their orientation phase of incarceration, Jason and Brandon were observed and evaluated by staff. The purpose of this monthlong procedure was to flush out any potential enemies or gang ties an inmate may have. The process is crucial for learning how to best protect the inmates. In state prisons, prisoners are separated by gang or race, or sometimes by crime, depending on what the safest situation will be. Since Jason and Brandon were only nineteen, and had no records or histories with anybody in the system, they had no threats; nor were they deemed threats to anyone else. As bad as SHU was for the human condition, "mainlining" or getting tossed into general population had its downsides as well, as they were about to learn.

THE YARD

AFTER THEIR ORIENTATION WEEKS IN THE SHU, Jason and Brandon were transitioned into a more modified facility in Salinas Valley State Prison. They looked forward to enjoying a more social yard where they could interact with other inmates during outside recreation time and actually soak up the sunlight or run real laps. More importantly, Jason and Brandon could finally commiserate. They both knew that their days in the same yard or even the same facility were numbered. Codefendants generally aren't allowed to stay housed together or communicate at all while incarcerated. Early on, while the two walked laps around the yard one day, Jason turned to Brandon with a serious face. He struggled to hide his shame. "I am so sorry," he said.

"Well," Brandon said, "we're here now. So let's just work on taking care of each other. We're family."

"Until death."

Within minutes, Brandon was approached by a brand-new inmate who was a member of a Mexican gang. The young man essentially said, "This is nothing personal. I've gotta put in work. And you're the target." He proceeded to whip a series of razor blades—which he had hidden between his teeth and cheeks—out of his mouth. Before Brandon could process what was happening, Jason bolted for the guy and tackled him to the ground. As Brandon jumped in between Jason and the thrashing blades, to protect him from being sliced, the brawl was abruptly halted by the deafening explosion of gunshots. Barrels of Ruger Mini-14 semiautomatic rifles emerged from several of the guard towers. The Mini-14 is known for shooting with extreme accuracy at long ranges, and its cartridge packs a high-level velocity of over three thousand feet per second and can penetrate Kevlar body armor. It's meant for two things: hunting and military combat. Stunned into paralysis, the three inmates huddled together and apologized to one another profusely. Brandon recalled that the blasts seemed to last forever. He said, "This is it. This is how it ends." Miraculously, none of the three was hit by the gunfire. Unfortunately, one of their friends, who was walking in an entirely different yard, wasn't so lucky. Several bullets ricocheted off steel poles and lodged into his neck. He survived. Barely.

Eventually the three inmates stood up, dusted themselves off, and simultaneously said, "Welcome to the yard."

ROLLING STONE

IN EARLY SEPTEMBER 1997, RANDALL SULLIVAN'S in-depth article on the case was published in *Rolling Stone* magazine. Sullivan said, "The story is as much about the community and communities like it all over the country, as it is about seven boys in a backyard brawl. The incident was local—the issue is national." Titled "Lynching in Malibu: A Tale of Fear, Retribution and Injustice in the War Against Youth," the article dissected the case in an objective look at the facts, and Sullivan interviewed just about everybody involved, with the notable exception of Mike McLoren. When Randall Sullivan talked with friends of all seven of the boys, they painted a much clearer picture of the history of these groups and the reality of their lives in Agoura Hills.

Honors student and popular good-girl Nicole Weinberg knew all the boys and had been close with Jason Holland since they were young. She had written several letters to *The Acorn*, the local

Valley newspaper, just after the trial in an attempt to set some of the story straight. In one of these letters she wrote, "Glorifying Jimmy Farris and portraying the aggressors as low-life trash was not only wrong but completely inaccurate. All of the boys concerned are good kids traveling on the wrong road. They are all victims and products of our environment."

Nicole described the Holland brothers to Randall Sullivan. Both very bright, their intelligence manifested in different ways. Although Micah was articulate and perceptive, he had difficulty concentrating and could barely get by, passing with Cs in school. Jason, however, could earn good grades without ever studying. "I was so envious of Jason back in the seventh grade," Nicole explained. "I was the big straight-A student. But I had to study hard. Jason would be joking around in the back of the class . . . but then he'd get a better grade on the test than I would." Both boys were small. Micah stood only five feet tall, and Jason less than six inches taller. And neither were big fighters. In fact, any scuffles Jason got into were only the result of stepping in when Micah got into trouble with his mouth. "Jason was always taking care of Micah—protecting him, covering up for him," Nicole said.

Dwayne Dahlberg, Johnny Vinnedge, and John Berardis, who were friends with both crews of boys and who had partied with most of them that day, expressed their frustration with how the media handled the story from the beginning. They were always convinced that the news agencies had an alliance with the police. John Berardis said, "In the news it was this 'clubhouse slaying' and 'gang killing,' like it was some kind of planned thing." Dwayne

Dahlberg added, "Everybody knew these kids were incapable of some cold-blooded killing. I was with them that day. We were all drinking together. And they weren't talking about any robbery. They went over to Mike's to get some weed, like everybody did. They were all drunk, and some shit happened, probably between Mike and Micah. It turned into a fight and somebody did a stupid thing, which was to pull a knife."

Dahlberg, Vinnedge, and Berardis, who had grown up with the victims and the defendants, shed some light on Mike's and Jimmy's backstories. What upset them most was the media's portrayal of McLoren and Jimmy as completely innocent victims. Never was there any mention of Mike McLoren being a dealer, which was annoying because according to them, absolutely everybody in town knew that McLoren's fort was *the* place to buy your drugs. He had the major hookup for all the good stuff. In Agoura Hills, "there are no secrets," Dahlberg said. "Everybody in this town knows everything about everybody else." According to Johnny Vinnedge, "The cops knew Mike was a dealer."

When it came to questions about Jimmy Farris, the boys were in total agreement. Berardis said, "There was no one who didn't know that the fort was where you went to get high. And Jimmy was there every day." Dwayne Dahlberg was brutally honest with Randall Sullivan: "Jimmy wasn't some angel. He wore all black all the time with this, like, satanic stuff on his leather jacket. Pentagrams and upside-down crosses and shit." John Berardis chimed in, "The guy was a grungy death rocker who wore fucking twenty-hole boots and twelve chains." Berardis was referring to the fact that Jimmy's combat boots and the rest of his attire was generally a fashion statement worn by teens who were into the occult and violence in the 1990s.

It wasn't that they had no sympathy for Jimmy Farris or Mike McLoren, but their opinion was that the two were just as big troublemakers as Jason, Micah, Brandon, Tony, and Chris. Everybody who knew Mike and Jimmy could see mayhem brewing with the antics that went down in that fort. Mike was weak but liked to cause trouble. He tried to improve his reputation and status by selling and giving away drugs. Because Jimmy was large, strong, and fearless, his role became McLoren's bodyguard, always around to protect against anybody who messed with Mike.

The best example of this was the Phil Hill incident. Phil Hill was one of the few black students at Agoura High School. According to his classmates, he was pretty harmless. Still, he talked a lot of smack, and every time somebody called him out on his bullying, he'd threaten to "whip some white ass." At six foot two, nobody wanted to take him up on his threat. About two years before Jimmy's death, Phil busted into some lockers at school one day. He stole some things from one of Jimmy's good friends, including a credit card. When Jimmy confronted him about it, Phil shouted, "Go fuck yourself." Jimmy waited outside his classroom, and when class was over, he punched Phil in the face. The story goes that he hit him with such force, Phil Hill was lifted off his feet and flew backward right into the air. Whether that part was true or not, Phil did end up in the hospital with his jaw broken in two places. Phil's mother, Lawanda, told reporters that the Farris family appeared at the hospital that night, Judie clutching a crucifix and crying while apologizing to the Hill family for her son's brutality. Judie was hysterical, and at one point she made an interesting offer. Since her son had harmed Phil so badly, she told Lawanda that she could "hurt her" as payback, to make things right. An eye-for-an-eye proposal was on the table. Lawanda did not hit Judie Farris. Jimmy was arrested for assault. But the charges were quickly dropped.

The incident actually helped Jimmy's status at school, because he was the first person to really deal with Phil in such a harsh way. People were tired of Phil Hill's threats. It helped Mike McLoren as well. Like John Berardis said, "Nobody liked him (McLoren). But he wasn't getting picked on anymore." After that Jimmy became known as "Peewee's bodyguard." Nobody called him that to his face, though.

APPEAL

IN JANUARY 2001, THE CALIFORNIA STATE COURT OF
Appeal finally rendered its decision on whether any legal errors
had occurred during the trial. First, evidence in the Alyce
Moulder Incident was discussed. It was the opinion of the
appeals attorneys that bringing up this incident was prejudicial
and inappropriate. The issue of the appellants' intent when they
entered Mike McLoren's fort was the entire crux of the case. Did
they drive over there to buy marijuana, or steal marijuana? The
answer to that question determined a manslaughter conviction
versus a first-degree murder conviction, and there was an enormous difference between the two in terms of the futures of the
four boys. A manslaughter conviction would have earned each of
them a few years in prison, at most. First-degree murder meant
forever.

The appellate attorneys claimed that Jason choosing to steal

Alyce Moulder's wallet did not prove that the other boys had larcenous intent as well that day. And just because he took a wallet, it did not automatically make him a thief in all other situations. The panel of appellate judges disagreed. "The Moulder Incident and the charged crimes are theft-type offenses involving group action and intimidating conduct by members of the group. The acting group consisted of all appellants. Finally, it occurred at a time and location relevant to the charged offenses." Also, "If a person acts similarly in similar situations, he probably harbors the same intent in each instance. Such prior conduct is relevant." The appellate panel concluded, "The court did not abuse its discretion."

The second issue dissected was the prosecution's improper use of the gang references. When Jeffrey Semow shouted at Jason Holland on the stand and repeatedly used the word "Gumbys," it was used as an unethical fear tactic that worked on the jury. Again, the appellate panel disagreed. Since Judge Mira had instructed the jury to pretend they'd never heard the gang discussion, Semow's antics were fine, not prejudicial at all. "The court did not abuse its discretion."

Juror misconduct was brought up. Specifically, Juror Number Three continually brought her twentysomething daughter to lunch with the other jurors. Juror Number Three's daughter also sat inside the courtroom for the entire nine weeks of the trial. Witnesses and the defendants saw the daughter speaking with the Farris family quite often. Who was this young woman? It came out later that she was, in fact, a good friend of Travis

Farris, Jimmy's older brother, and she knew Judie and Jim as well. Juror Number Three was also the person that Juror Number Ten had seen embracing Mike McLoren and the Farris family immediately after the trial. She should never have been on that jury. When questioned in jury selection, Juror Number Three should have admitted to having ties to the victims, and would have therefore been excused immediately because of bias. No problem, the appellate judges said. They expressed that they had investigated the situation and both the mother and daughter promised that they never discussed any details of the case with anybody during the nine weeks. Ever. Therefore, "The court did not abuse its discretion."

After stating, "Substantial evidence supports the felony murder convictions of all four appellants," the panel had some final thoughts. "The evidence regarding Anthony Miliotti's role in the events at the fort was conflicting." Had Tony actually acted with reckless indifference to human life? After all, there was no evidence that Tony participated in the Alyce Moulder Incident, and Mike McLoren could only ever place Tony standing in the doorway to his fort. Jason, Brandon, and Micah were all participants in the fight. All had criminal records. In fact, Micah, the youngest, already had a rap sheet listing burglary, vandalism, battery, and runaway. Therefore, there was no doubt that "Micah was headed in a direction of serious criminality." Tony, on the other hand, had no record at all.

In the end, the appellate panel of judges concluded, "We find as a matter of law that the evidence is insufficient to support a finding that Miliotti was a major participant in the attempted robbery or burglary or that he acted with a reckless indifference to human life." Tony's conviction was changed to murder in the second degree. His sentence was reduced, and he would be eligible for parole. Someday.

CRIMINAL ED

BY THE TIME BRANDON, JASON, AND MICAH HAD
settled into life in prison, the new millennium had arrived. But
the United States seemed to be moving backward with respect to
criminal justice. Though the country held only 5 percent of the
planet's population, America contained 20 percent of the world's
incarcerated. Within the previous twenty years, the prison
population had almost quadrupled. The Ronald Reagan era of the
1980s revolved around being "tough on crime." As a result of the
overcrowding of US prisons, those on the inside began to develop
highly organized gangs with specific rules and expectations to
maintain order within the chaos.

After his first year incarcerated in Los Angeles County Men's
Central Jail, Brandon had learned enough to understand exactly
what the drill would be once he was tossed into the big house.
Generally, units and yards were separated by gang. Soon after

arriving, inmates were expected to choose an affiliation. Gang leaders literally asked for paperwork, criminal files, and all documented information in an inmate's possession. A new prisoner proved his loyalty by "putting in work" immediately. That work could include slicing somebody, stealing something, or carrying kites for the members. *Kites* is prison lingo for hand-scrawled notes. Most information between prisoners is communicated through kites, which are illegal. Still, massive daily transferring of kites is what keeps the order in prisons. In Brandon's case, the veteran inmates who approached him in those first days were in for the surprise of their lives.

During the last conversation he had with his father before the long hiatus on visits, Brandon said, "Dad, don't worry about me. I'm prepared for this. I'm just going to do the best I possibly can." It turns out, Brandon's philosophy on surviving prison worked well for him. It helped that he was smart and emotionally strong—some would say stoic. And, ironically, he had an unshakable desire to stay out of trouble. Brandon remembered being scared of his environment, naturally, but he was more afraid of losing himself and his core morals. After all, drinking, tooling around, and acting reckless had culminated in a first-degree murder conviction and life in prison. Aside from drinking underage, he had not even broken a major law or killed anybody. And he wasn't about to start.

In fact, during Brandon's first week at Salinas Valley State Prison, he pulled a trick that few, if any, had attempted before. When it was suggested that he put in work for a Caucasian group, he simply refused. The old-timer who was assigned to approach him informed Brandon that he would have to be punished by getting stabbed, maybe killed. The first thing everybody learned in prison was that you either do what you are told immediately, or you get hurt. Brandon opened his arms wide and basically said, *Go ahead. Do what you need to. I'm not going to fight back. I'm in here for a murder I didn't do. And I sure as fuck am not going to get in trouble for murdering somebody for real. Do it. I really don't care.* The thing about being locked up, even for only a year, is that the environment can create sort of a numb depression in some people. For Brandon, his life was over. He was sentenced to die in prison. And sometimes he felt like the sooner, the better.

Brandon wasn't stabbed. He had taken an enormous risk, a life-threatening one. But he had impressed the old-timers. They respected his conviction. He found that the more he said no to other inmates, the more respect he gained. They probably just didn't know what to make of this small, handsome young man. His unorthodox methods were unprecedented. Eventually, Brandon's role became one of a willing scapegoat. Because he was serving a life sentence without the possibility of parole, he could afford to take the fall for other inmates when they got into trouble. He certainly wouldn't take a murder rap. But he would keep his mouth shut if he witnessed anything suspicious. He'd get tossed into the hole time and time again for infractions he had nothing to do with. And the other inmates loved him for it. When cells were "tossed," or rummaged by the guards looking for contraband, he alleged that all weapons belonged to him.

And if he was questioned about a crime, he claimed ignorance. This was Brandon's game plan. Protect others. Take abuse even if you don't deserve it. Don't snitch. Ever. Instill trust. Rather than joining one gang or clique, Brandon somehow befriended all of them.

One time, Brandon saw his cellie smuggling in a large nail he had found out in the yard. They argued over whether his cell mate should get rid of it. Brandon tried reasoning with him, reminding him that if anybody found the contraband, they were both in trouble. When Brandon tried to grab it from him, his roommate threw it into their vent. It was stuck. And they couldn't retrieve it. Eventually the guards tossed the cells, as they often did, and found the nail. Instead of just letting the guards take both of them to SHU, Brandon claimed it was his nail. His cellie had no clue he had hidden it, he said. He begged the guards not to write up his friend. He reminded them that his cellie had a parole date coming up in a month. Why would a guy so close to release hide a weapon in his air vent? Brandon spent a week in SHU. His cellie left one month later, indebted for life.

Over the years, Brandon witnessed endless fights, stabbings, and murders. One of the most frightening events occurred when he and three friends sat on a table in the yard, eating Popsicles. Brandon held a cup of Coke in his hand. While he was passing the cup to his friend so he could scoop some ice out, another inmate approached from behind, grabbed his friend by the hair on the back of his head, and slashed his throat. His companion was inches away from him, with his hand still on the Coke.

Brandon's hand was literally touching his friend's when he watched the other guy collapse.

Over the course of twenty years, Brandon was transferred all over the state of California, and he served time in every maximum-security prison. The justice system likes to move inmates around, most likely so they don't get too comfortable in one spot. By a miracle, Brandon survived without any fights or serious disciplinary reports, called 115's in California. He did, however, enjoy heroin, as most inmates do. After a "dirty" random drug test several years into his incarceration, he quit cold turkey. Despite all his time in SHU after taking the blame for other inmates' infractions, he was always cleared of charges, probably because the staff knew he was covering for somebody else. And, because Brandon was so likable, even the guards respected his philosophy on surviving prison.

An exceptionally talented artist, Brandon spent most of his time painting, sketching, and perfecting his prison tattoo methods. Soon he became one of the most sought-after ink artists in the system. He did the ink for free, because he loved the process and it gave him purpose. This was another tool in his belt that enhanced his likability and chances for survival. Even the staff in the facilities marveled at how one kid, thrown into the system at age eighteen, could survive so many years unscathed and with a relatively clean record. It was extremely rare.

Jason and Micah spent much of their first decade in prison on lockdown in SHU at various facilities, and for various reasons.

Around 2004, they were both locked up in the same cell-block at Corcoran State Prison. On lockdown twenty-three hours per day, they never spoke or touched. They hadn't seen each other or communicated since 1996. State prisoners are forbidden from writing letters to other inmates in the state, and they certainly cannot talk by phone. Jason was fortunate to be placed in the middle cell of the SHU facility, and he could see Micah's reflection in his corner cell through a conveniently placed glass partition by the guard office. So he was able to watch his beloved little brother grow up into a man, at least in mirror image.

For the next ten years, Jason and Micah communicated through kites that were transferred via "fishing lines" they created using the tiny elastic threads pulled from state-issued boxer shorts. "Fishing" refers to the crafty way inmates transfer items and information via lines sent through air vents, under cell door cracks, and even through the toilets. Jason became a master fisherman, so adept at creating seamless, almost invisible elastic lines of staggering length, his "job" became the Corcoran SHU cell-block postmaster. Jason learned to transport just about anything through his ingenious lines and weights. Kites, legal documents, writing implements, magazines, family photos, even burritos, were no match for his MacGyver-esque skills. When asked how in the world he could possibly accomplish all that from a ten-square-foot cell with few supplies, Jason—now a self-taught engineer—responded, "All we had was time. What else were we going to do in there?"

AFTERMATH

YEARS FLEW BY. INTEREST IN THE CASE WAXED AND waned. Still, Randall Sullivan's comprehensive *Rolling Stone* article created a ripple effect, one that cannot be minimized. The general public was outraged after the story was given international attention from Sullivan's skilled perspective. He took what could have been chalked up as another "super-predator" killing in suburban America and dissected it for what it really was. California Case Number SA022108 was never a first-degree murder case. It was manslaughter, plain and simple. It was never a robbery; nor was the killing of Jimmy Farris intentional. One boy made a stupid decision. Four boys paid the ultimate price. Five, counting Chris Velardo. Five years in the California Youth Authority system is no picnic. Fortunately for him, Velardo was released in the year 2000, and went on to build a massively successful career as an art director, primarily in the advertising world. The decision to take a deal, plead guilty, and avoid a trial was the best choice Chris Velardo could have made. Had Jason, Micah, Brandon, and Tony been granted the same leniency as Chris, there is little doubt that all four of them would be highly successful members of society today.

Many people believed the boys were punished with the harshest sentence not for what they did, but for who was killed. One cannot underestimate the power of a grieving father, who happens to be a treasured police officer. A homicide detective, no less. Jim Farris Senior, however, has always maintained that he had no influence on how the case was handled.

Critics of the convictions and sentences argue that the entire case was also politically maneuvered by an embarrassed district attorney's office that desperately needed a conviction. They had just lost two major internationally broadcast cases that should have been slam-dunk wins—the Menendez murder case and the O. J. Simpson double homicide. The O. J. Simpson murder trial was the most publicized criminal trial in American history, according to *USA Today*. Simpson, the charismatic and beloved National Football League star, was arrested and charged with the savage June 1994 stabbing murder of his ex-wife, Nicole Brown Simpson, and her friend Ronald Goldman. With a documented history of spousal abuse and an enormous mountain of evidence pointing only to O. J. Simpson as the killer, the district attorney's office believed they undoubtedly had means, motive, and opportunity covered in this open-and-shut case. However, the eleven-month melodrama of a trial—televised for all the world to see—presented unexpected twists and turns that buried the prosecution's case. When the jury delivered a not guilty verdict on October 3, 1995, Los Angeles District Attorney Gil Garcetti and his team of prosecutors suffered irrevocable embarrassment.

Although worldwide use of the Internet was still relatively tiny, Gene Hein took it upon himself to ride the wave of renewed attention given to the case after Randall Sullivan's article was published. Gene vowed to make things right no matter how long it took. Just before the year 2000, Gene created a website, BrandonHeinArt.com. The site featured artwork Brandon created in prison over the years, photos, and a description of the story with links to news articles. Gene's relentless efforts in bringing attention to the case of the Agoura Four, and Randall Sullivan's heavy involvement in the case, eventually spawned a documentary called *Reckless Indifference*, created by Academy Award–nominated and Emmy Award–winning producer/director William Gazecki.

In the film, Gazecki and California senator Thomas Hayden interview a frightened twenty-one-year-old Brandon Hein from the Pelican Bay State Prison. Situated in Northern California up by the Oregon border, Pelican Bay is the only supermax prison in the state. Super-maximum-security facilities contain the highest level of control and virtually zero independence for inmates. Boasting the "worst of the worst" inmates and providing absolutely appalling conditions, the facility has experienced more riots, killings, and hunger strikes than most others in the country. Brandon had no idea how he ended up there. Word was, if some authority in the system got the green light to torture an inmate, they were woken up and strapped to a bus heading to Pelican Bay. Soon after Brandon arrived, he heard that Jason was there as well. Somebody in the system was undoubtedly abusing power and aimed to punish them to the full extent of the law.

Like Randall Sullivan's *Rolling Stone* article, *Reckless Indifference* featured almost every single person involved in the case, from attorneys to families, friends, and community members. Even law enforcement weighed in. A former Los Angeles sheriff went on record to state his exasperation with how Jason, Micah, Brandon, and Tony had been unapologetically railroaded by a corrupt system in order to make an example out of them and send a wake-up call to troubled boys.

After wrapping up filming, Thomas Hayden told Brandon, "Thank you for speaking with us. If there is ever anything I can do for you, please let me know." Brandon replied immediately. "Yeah. Get me the *fuck* out of Pelican Bay." And Hayden did. Immediately.

Soon news crews came calling. In 2003 the CBS show *60 Minutes*, the longest-running news show in the country, featured the case of Brandon, Jason, Micah, and Tony. Dan Rather interviewed Jason and Brandon on-screen and brought major worldwide attention to their plight and the realities of the felony murder rule. Senator Hayden used the news programming and the *Reckless Indifference* documentary as a springboard for drafting a bill that would eliminate, or at least reform, California's felony murder rule. Unfortunately, his bill died in the Senate.

APPEAL AGAIN

IN 2001, TONY MILIOTTI HAD WON A SMALL VICTORY when the boys' attorneys successfully had his conviction reduced from first-degree murder to manslaughter during the appeals process on the state level. Nine years later, the boys had one more shot at freedom during the federal appeals process. In April 2010, the United States Ninth Circuit Court of Appeals listened to oral arguments led by appeals attorney William Genego, who was hired by Brandon Hein. Attorneys discovered that the prosecution in the case had committed what is called a Brady violation. That is, Jeffrey Semow and Michael Latin purposefully withheld information from the defense team that could have affected the outcome of the trial. In the tens of thousands of documents filed on the case, a one-page letter was found. Specifically, a July 10, 1995, letter from the DA's office showed that Mike McLoren had been given total immunity from prosecution for possessing and selling drugs. In exchange, he gave his testimony and the robbery story they needed to convict the boys of felony murder. Had the defense known about this at the time, they would have brought it out on cross-examination. The jury's feeling about Mike McLoren's honesty in this case would have been destroyed. This was huge. Usually when a Brady violation is found, a conviction is overturned. Prosecutors are simply not allowed to hide important information like that.

Could this one letter from July 1995, which was buried among thousands of documents, be the key to finally set Jason, Micah, Brandon, and Tony free? William Genego, a tireless warrior of justice, weaved through the complexities of the wrongdoings in the case and argued passionately for hours. At times the panel of three federal appellate judges completely agreed with him. They seemed almost surprised that the prosecutors had gotten away with such shenanigans.

Unfortunately, in the end, the very conservative three-judge panel decided not to show mercy. They ultimately ruled that, yes, there was a Brady violation, and that was too bad. Sorry. After evaluating all the case records, they came to the conclusion that even if that information had come out at trial, the jury probably would still have convicted all four boys of murder in the first degree. Sadly, we'll never know. By April 2010, all appeals had been exhausted. There was no more hope.

Or was there?

Brandon's one shot was a miracle that only the governor of the State of California could perform. Through the persistence of friends and family members, Brandon gathered commutation papers and submitted them to Governor Arnold Schwarzenegger's office, along with hundreds of letters of support. Because he had been convicted at such a young age and had a largely impeccable prison record, Brandon seemed the most likely to have a shot at a reduction in his sentence. It was a last-ditch effort, one that historically rarely paid off. Most governors didn't see a point to looking soft on crime. Still, Schwarzenegger was fairly liberal. More importantly, he was about to leave office. Eventually, William Gazecki's documentary *Reckless Indifference* made it into the hands of Governor Arnold Schwarzenegger. He was moved. So moved, in fact, that he made a bold statement. He removed the "Without Parole" portion of Brandon's sentence. Brandon would still be serving a life sentence in prison, but now with a possibility of parole. Brandon would be eligible for parole in 2020, the same year as Micah Holland.

Finally, Brandon Hein had a small chance at freedom.

PAROLE

IN THE YEAR 2011, SIXTEEN YEARS AFTER JIMMY Farris's death, thirty-three-year-old Tony Miliotti finally had his shot at freedom. The parole board looked for maturity, taking responsibility for one's part in a crime, and especially a release plan. Tony had no such plan. The board could not release a prisoner unless he had at least one solid job offer, a documented place to live—either transitional housing or a family home—and a five-year plan for staying sober and crime free. Both Tony's father and aunt had passed away by then. Most of his family had moved out of state, and communication was sporadic and strained, as often happens when people are locked up for decades. Tony had nowhere to live upon release. He also did not have a plan for income or a job waiting for him. Without solid family and community support, and some steady source of money, parole becomes virtually impossible.

Tony was denied parole. The board hoped that he could have another hearing in ten years, the year 2021. He would be forty-three years old.

LIFE IS NOT FAIR

DECADES HAVE PASSED. FAMILIES HAVE SUFFERED.
Lives were destroyed. All because of a drunken backyard
fight, and one momentary lapse in judgment. Not a single
day passes that Jason, Brandon, Micah, and Tony don't feel
regret. They are haunted by their contributions to the loss of
Jimmy Farris's life.

Jason and Micah Holland were finally reunited in Kern Valley
State Prison in 2015. They were fortunate to share a cell and live
together for the first time since they were teenagers. After suffering in SHU for a decade, they relished the luxury of having
occasional contact visits with friends and family, where they were
allowed one hug from each person upon arrival. Jason is a vora-
cious reader and spends his free time teaching GED preparation
classes to fellow inmates. He is especially adept at teaching math
skills, algebra in particular. Although they have never had access

to computers, cellular phones, or the Internet, Jason has become a loyal follower of the Tony Robbins philosophies through reading his books. A businessman, bestselling author, and philanthropist, Tony Robbins has established himself as the world's self-help guru. His charitable foundation provides programming for schools, prisons, the elderly, and homeless facilities with the belief that "regardless of stature, only those who have learned the power of sincere and selfless contribution experience life's deepest joy; true fulfillment." Jason dreams of taking the self-help principles he's studied and applying them in prisons as an instructor.

Now middle-aged, regardless of the cards they were dealt, both Jason and Micah have adopted lifestyles of optimism and productivity. They have taken and excelled in a number of college-level courses. During intensive weekly creative writing classes, both men have developed advanced skills in crafting fiction and nonfiction short stories. They are also naturally gifted artists, painting and sketching still life, abstract, and portrait pieces when they have access to art supplies. During their one contact visit per month (the other weekend visits are limited to thirty minutes behind the glass using a corded phone), Jason chats with his guests while continuously creating intricate origami animals for fellow inmates' toddler children, who are relentless in their demands for his attention. When kids of inmates grow restless during seven-hour visits, confined to one small cafeteria with no toys, play structures, or anywhere to run, Micah becomes the entertainment relief, telling funny jokes and stories while sharing M&M's from his vending machine trail mix.

Brandon Hein has remained free of any disciplinary reports. He spends his time counseling young inmates, leading substance abuse treatment groups, and yearns to teach painting and tattoo artistry to teens someday on the outside. He creates haunting paintings and sketches—also still life, abstract, and portraits—that his father, Gene, sells through an online gallery and in art shows. A natural leader, Brandon spearheaded the mural project at Lancaster State Prison and guided a team of inmates in creating an enormous outdoor mural on the wall of C-Unit featuring a bald eagle embracing a rippling American flag. Unfortunately, Brandon was unexpectedly moved from Lancaster to Pleasant Valley State Prison just before the mural was completed. In January 2016 he sent a letter to his father that was posted on a Facebook site dedicated to Brandon. He signed off by saying, "I was transferred days before I was able to complete my side (all I had left was the stars). But all in all it was a good experience for me, and my two mural buddies "Vinnie" and "Spike" were two friends I'll always remember. Being outside, listening to music, and painting all day is definitely something I love doing (even on a prison yard!) and WILL do someday as a free man!"

Many supporters of Jason, Micah, Brandon, and Tony feel like they've paid their dues. They've become better people. They have all four grown into mature, intelligent, productive middle-aged men. They pose no threat to society. Life in prison is not fair. They've done enough time.

Others, however, agree with the words of Judie Farris:

"How much time is enough time . . . for taking a life?"

ACKNOWLEDGMENTS

Thank you to my sister and best friend, Amy—public defender extraordinaire—for helping me every step of the way through researching this haunting story. My parents, Madre and Padre Porinchak, also provided unparalleled support. You are officially the greatest family ever!

Thank you to the Simon & Schuster (Simon Pulse) team for taking a chance on this new genre of criminal justice nonfiction for young adults, and certainly for taking a chance on me. Fiona Simpson, Mara Anastas, and Elisa Rivlin: I am honored to launch the Simon True line with you lovely ladies. Cheers!

Jill Corcoran, my longtime friend and agency partner, this book would never have been possible without you proudly bringing up my work with the incarcerated to anybody who will listen. Your dedication to me, and support for my career, mean the world to me.

A giant thank-you to Gene Hein, Sharry Holland, Melissa Page, William Genego, William Gazecki, Scott Budnick, Randall Sullivan, Karen Baxter, and Nicole Weinberg for taking time to chat with me about all these difficult memories. Through all your efforts, the world of criminal justice is finally beginning to change so that our young people are treated with some dignity. Perhaps someday punishments will more appropriately fit the crimes.

Michael Latin and Linda Triano—I so appreciate you keeping me grounded with your perspectives. This story is such a tragedy all the way around. And none of us will forget that Jimmy and the Farris family paid the ultimate price for somebody else's poor judgment. My hope is that this story can help prevent a similar future incident.

Last, I am forever grateful to Jason Holland, Micah Holland, and Brandon Hein for allowing me into their lives. Your remorse and kind words about Jimmy move me to tears. And I marvel at your ability to stay positive and productive, even in the most heinous of environments. I sincerely hope we'll all meet around a table for beers someday . . . on the outs.

SOURCES

Newspaper Articles

Riccardi, Nicholas, and Abigail Goldman. "3 Held in Fatal Agoura Hills Stabbing." *Los Angeles Times*, May 24, 1995, Metro Part B, Valley edition.

Riccardi, Nicholas, and Tracy Wilson. "Minors Held in Stabbings May Be Tried as Adults." *Los Angeles Times*, May 25, 1995.

Moran, Julio. "Agoura Hills: Man Denied Guilt in Slaying of Youth." *Los Angeles Times*, May 26, 1995.

Riccardi, Nicholas. "Family Mourns Boy, 16, Killed in Stabbing." *Los Angeles Times*, May 27, 1995, Valley edition.

Riccardi, Nicholas. "Attorneys Challenge Prosecution's Version of Stabbing of Youth; Violence: Lawyers Contend the Death of an Agoura Hills Teenager Resulted from a Drug Deal Gone Wrong, Not Robbery." *Los Angeles Times*, May 31, 1995.

Slater, Eric. "4th Suspect Arrested in Boy's Death; Calabasas: The 17-Year-Old Is Thought to Have Been Present When James Farris III, 16, Was Stabbed. He Surrenders to Deputies and Is Booked into Juvenile Hall." *Los Angeles Times*, June 3, 1995.

Riccardi, Nicholas. "17-Year-Old Is 5th Youth Charged in Stabbing Death." *Los Angeles Times*, June 7, 1995, Valley edition.

Reed, Mack. "Oak Park Teenager Ordered to Face Trial in Murder, Robbery Case; Stabbing: The 18-Year-Old Is Charged in the Death of James Farris III of Agoura Hills." *Los Angeles Times*, June 8, 1995.

Blechman, Andrew D. "Fugitive, 18, Surrenders to Police in Clubhouse Slaying. Crime: Accompanied by His mother, Jason Holland of Thousand Oaks Turns Himself In. He Was Wanted for the Knifing of an Agoura Hills Teenager." *Los Angeles Times*, June 12, 1995.

Chen, Vivian Lou. "7 Arrested in Slaying of Taft High Student Outside West Hills Theater. Crime: Suspects Range in Age from 15–19." *Los Angeles Times*, June 12, 1995.

Moran, Julio. "Hearing Delayed for 3 Youths in Stabbing." *Los Angeles Times*, June 17, 1995.

Harris, Scott. "To a Mother, the Enemy Is Violence." *Los Angeles Times*, June 22, 1995, Metro, Part B.

Manning, Frank. "Agoura Hills: Meeting to Focus on Teenage Violence." *Los Angeles Times*, June 24, 1995.

Brommer, Stephanie. "3 Teenagers Face Trial as Adults in Slaying. Crime: Two Are from Ventura County. Life Terms Are Possible in the Stabbing Death of an Agoura Hills Boy and Wounding of Another." *Los Angeles Times*, July 28, 1995, Ventura West edition.

Brommer, Stephanie. "3 Teenagers Ordered to Stand Trial in Slaying. Crime: Defendants Will be Prosecuted as Adults in Death of a 16-Year-Old Boy and the Wounding of Another in Agoura Hills." *Los Angeles Times*, August 18, 1995.

Pols, Mary F. "5 Youths Will Stand Trial Together in Fatal Stabbing." *Los Angeles Times*, August 19, 1995, Metro, Part B.

Pols, Mary F. "Oak Park/Thousand Oaks: Death Penalty Waived in Teen Murder Trial." *Los Angeles Times*, September 14, 1995, East Ventura County Focus.

Pols, Mary F. "Agoura Hills: Defendants in Teen's Slaying Separated." *Los Angeles Times*, September 16, 1995, Metro, Part B.

Pols, Mary F. "Teen Pleads to Manslaughter in Stabbing Death. Courts: Chris Velardo Had No Direct Role in Slaying, Prosecutor Says. Four Others Face Trial in the Death of 16-Year-Old Agoura Hills Resident." *Los Angeles Times*, September 29, 1995.

Pols, Mary F. "Murder Trial of 4 Teens Postponed. Courts: Defense in Stabbing Death of 16-Year-Old Claims New Evidence Left It Unprepared. Judge Grants Continuance Until Jan. 8." *Los Angeles Times*, October 7, 1995.

Manning, Frank. "Agoura Hills: Task Force Will Offer Ideas to Stem Violence." *Los Angeles Times*, October 16, 1995, Metro, Part B.

Pols, Mary F. "Tale of Death, Intrigue Jars Quiet Agoura Hills." *Los Angeles Times*, October 22, 1995, Part A, Zones Desk.

Pols, Mary F. "Suburban Wanna-Be Gang Gets Attention of Authorities. Behavior: Police Say the Gumbys, the Group Allegedly 'Claimed' by One of Five Friends Held in Slaying, Generally Stick to Smaller Crimes." *Los Angeles Times*, October 22, 1995, Part A, Zones Desk.

Pols, Mary F. "Jury Selection to Begin in 4 Teens' Death Trial." *Los Angeles Times*, February 27, 1996, Ventura County edition.

Pols, Mary F. "Prosecutors Press for Gang Link in Trial of Four Conejo Teens." *Los Angeles Times*, March 19, 1996.

Coit, Michael. "Trial to Start Today in Death of Agoura Teen." *Daily News* (Los Angeles), March 19, 1996.

Pols, Mary F. "Conejo Valley: Credibility of Gang Expert Is Under Fire." *Los Angeles Times*, March 20, 1996, Ventura County edition.

Coit, Michael. "Conejo Valley Briefly: Judge Postpones Trial in Teenager's Slaying." *Daily News* (Los Angeles), March 20, 1996.

Coit, Michael. "Court Considering Gang Evidence." *Daily News* (Los Angeles), March 22, 1996.

Pols, Mary F. "Conejo Valley: Murder Trial Judge Limits Gang Evidence." *Los Angeles Times*, March 26, 1996, Ventura County edition.

Coit, Michael. "Trial Starts in Death of Agoura Hills Teen." *Daily News* (Los Angeles), March 27, 1996.

Pols, Mary F. "Prosecutors Open Case Against 4 Teens Accused in Slaying." *Los Angeles Times*, March 27, 1996.

Coit, Michael. "Teens Studied Yard Prior to Attack, Witness Says." *Daily News* (Los Angeles), March 29, 1996.

Coit, Michael. "Agoura Stabbing Lures Noted Lawyers. Teens' Attorneys Used to Clients Like Lyle Menendez, Stacey Koon." *Daily News* (Los Angeles), March 31, 1996.

Coit, Michael. "Survivor to Testify About Stabbing." *Daily News* (Los Angeles), April 15, 1996.

Coit Michael. "Marijuana Shared in Fort, Girl Testifies." *Daily News* (Los Angeles), April 17, 1996.

Coit, Michael. "Stabbing Victim Testifies. Old Agoura Teen Details Attack, Friend's Death." *Daily News* (Los Angeles), April 18, 1996.

Pols, Mary F. "Credibility of Witness Assailed in Teens' Murder Trial." *Los Angeles Times*, April 19, 1996.

Coit, Michael. "Surviving Victim's Credibility Attacked in Teen Killing Trial." *Daily News* (Los Angeles), April 19, 1996.

Coit, Michael. "Alternate Juror Pool Dwindling in Trial of Teens." *Daily News* (Los Angeles), April 23, 1996.

Coit, Michael. "Defense Attorney Says Client Attacked by One of Stabbing Victims." *Daily News* (Los Angeles), April 23, 1996.

Coit, Michael. "Defendant Admits to Stabbing. Court Told Killing Was an Accident." *Daily News* (Los Angeles), May 1, 1996.

Coit, Michael. "Defense Focuses on Survivor in Stabbing." *Daily News* (Los Angeles), May 9, 1996.

Coit, Michael. "Deliberations Delayed in Teen Homicide Trial." *Daily News* (Los Angeles), May 11, 1996.

Pols, Mary F. "Jury Gets Case on Slaying of Area Youth." *Los Angeles Times*, May 11, 1996. Metro, Part B.

Coit, Michael. "Four Teens Convicted in Agoura Hills Murder." *Daily News* (Los Angeles), May 29, 1996.

Pols, Mary F. "Jury Convicts Teenagers in '95 Slaying of 16-Year-Old." *Los Angeles Times*, May 29, 1996, Metro, Part B, Zones Desk.

Pols, Mary F. "Killers' Mother Questions Fairness of Life Sentences." *Los Angeles Times*, July 15, 1996.

Pols, Mary F. "Sentencing of Teen's Killers Delayed." *Los Angeles Times*, July 15, 1996, Metro, Part B, Zones Desk.

Pols, Mary F. "Wrongful Death Suit Names Slain Teenager's Friend and His Family." *Los Angeles Times*, August 3, 1996, Metro, Part B, Zones Desk.

Coit, Michael. "Judge Denies Motions in Clubhouse Killing." *Daily News* (Los Angeles), August 20, 1996.

Pols, Mary F. "Teen's Killers Were Abused by Stepfather, Mother Says." *Los Angeles Times*, August 20, 1996, Metro, Part B, Zones Desk.

Pols, Mary F. "Relatives Plead for Teens Guilty in Slaying." *Los Angeles Times*, August 21, 1996, Metro, Part B, Zones Desk.

Coit, Michael. "Mercy Sought for 4 Convicted of Killing Teen." *Daily News* (Los Angeles), August 21, 1996.

Pols, Mary F. "4 Teens Get Maximum Sentences in Slaying." *Los Angeles Times*, August 22, 1996.

Coit, Michael. "Four Teens Get Life Sentences. Parole Ruled Out for 3 in Murder of LAPD Officer's Son." *Daily News* (Los Angeles), August 22, 1996.

Coit, Michael. "Pleas for Justice, Mercy Split Crowd Outside Courtroom." *Daily News* (Los Angeles), August 22, 1996.

Coit, Michael. "Teen Gets 11 Years in Agoura Killing." *Daily News* (Los Angeles), September 7, 1996.

Pols, Mary F. "Oak Park: Teen Gets 11 Years in Stabbing Death." *Los Angeles Times*, September 7, 1996, Metro, Part B, Zones Desk.

Coit, Michael. "Slayers' Families Miss Jailed Teenagers. Relatives Call Terms Too Harsh for Four." *Daily News* (Los Angeles), September 8, 1996.

Detrich, Dick. "The Wrong Place, Time, and Sentence." *Los Angeles Times*, April 6, 1997, Metro, Part B, Zones Desk, Ventura County edition.

Reed, Mack. "Imprisoned Killer Seeks Mercy Via Internet." *Los Angeles Times*, July 17, 1997.

Martinez, Al. "A Murder in Paradise." *Los Angeles Times*, March 12, 1999, Metro, Part B.

Talez, Margaret. "Scars and Bars. Tragedy: Jimmy Farris' Slaying in Agoura Hills Four Years Ago Shattered the Lives of His Parents and the Parents of Five Teens Imprisoned for the Crime." *Los Angeles Times*, July 25, 1995, Metro, Part B, Zones Desk.

Talev, Margaret. "Shock Gives Way to Hope Then Doubt for 1 of the 5." *Los Angeles Times*, July 25, 1999.

Fausset, Richard. "Movie on Teens' Roles in Slaying to Debut. 'Reckless Indifference' Documents Legal Aftermath of Stabbing Death of Agoura Hills Boy." *Los Angeles Times*, October 20, 2000.

Talev, Margaret. "Murder Case Appeal, Film Stir Tension." *Los Angeles Times*, December 3, 2000.

Loesing, John. "Appeals Underway in Local Murder Case." *The Acorn*, December 14, 2000.

Manzano, Roberto J. "Ventura County News: 3 Convictions in Teen's Slaying Upheld." *Los Angeles Times*, January 30, 2001.

Jaramillo Rushing, Rocky. "Valley Perspective. Perspective on Juvenile Justice: Tragic Slaying, Tragic Sentencing." *Los Angeles Times*, February 11, 2001, Metro, Part B.

Loesing, John. "Sentence Reduction Possible in Jimmy Farris Murder Case." *The Acorn*, February 15, 2001.

Loesing, John. "Attorney of Man Convicted in Local Murder Case Seeks a New Trial." *The Acorn*, February 13, 2003.

Martinez, Al. "Dad Holds Hope for Imprisoned Son." *Los Angeles Times*, November 17, 2006, Calendar, Part E.

Bertholdo, Stephanie. "1995 Agoura Murder Case Lives On." *The Acorn*, December 4, 2008.

Okamoto, Sherri M. "Court: State's Nondisclosure of Immunity Deal Not Prejudicial." *Metropolitan News-Enterprise*, April 13, 2010.

Kline, Breann. "Teen Murder Caused Broken Hearts, Broken Lives." *The Acorn*, July 1, 2010.

Books

Lane, Bryan, and Wilfred Gregg. *The Encyclopedia of Serial Killers*. New York: Berkley Books, 1995, pages 63, 64, 226.

Magazines

Dilulio, John J. "The Coming of the Super-Predators." *The Weekly Standard*, November 27, 1995. http://www.weeklystandard.com/the-coming-of-the-super-predators/article/8160.

Sullivan, Randall. "Lynching in Malibu: A Tale of Fear, Retribution and Injustice in the War Against Youth." *Rolling Stone*, September 4, 1997, pages 45–62 and 78–81.

Internet Articles

Cult Education Institute, CultEducation.com, "Mountain Park Baptist Church and Boarding Academy."

Goulding, Joan. "Freeway Killer Suspect William Bonin." UPI Archives, November 4, 1981. http://www.upi.com/Archives/1981/11/04/Freeway-killer-suspect-William-Bonin-was-a-man-with/3420373698000.

Websites

BrandonHeinArt.com

Network54.com
(http://www.network54.com/Forum/250687/thread/1053300915/1/

Welcome+Feel+Free+to+tell+the+truth+about+Mountain+Park+
Baptist+Church+%26amp%3B+Boarding+Academy. "Welcome. Feel Free
to Tell the Truth About Mountain Park Baptist Church and Boarding
Academy." Thread: *It's Okay, They Can't Hurt You Anymore* . . . May 18, 2003–
June 13, 2010.

Court Documents/Trial Transcripts/Appeals Transcripts

*The People of the State of California Versus Brandon Wade Hein, Jason Skip
Holland, Micah Holland, Anthony Miliotti, and Christopher Velardo. Case
#SA022108.* Volumes 1–56. October 11, 1996.

Court of Appeal, Second District, Division 7, California.

*The PEOPLE, Plaintiff and Respondent, v. Brandon Wade HEIN, et al.,
Defendants and Appellants.*

No. B106689. Decided: January 29, 2001

United States Court of Appeals for the Ninth Circuit. *HEIN Versus
SULLIVAN.* No. 07-56277, No. 07-56288, No. 07-56365, No. 07-56367.
Argued and Submitted October 7, 2009, Pasadena, California. Filed April
12, 2010. Opinion by Judge Trager, United States District Judge.

Documentary Film

Reckless Indifference. Directed by William Gazecki and Dale Rosenbloom,
featuring Brandon Hein and Alan Dershowitz, Utopia Films and Open Edge
Media, 2000.

Television

Life in Prison. Two-Part Television Documentary. Dan Rather, *60 Minutes*,
CBS, 2003.

The Superpredator Scare. Retro Report for the *New York Times*,
http://www.nytimes.com/video, April 6, 2014.

Interviews

Sharry Holland (mother of Jason and Micah Holland)

Jason Holland

Micah Holland

Brandon Hein

Gene Hein (father of Brandon Hein)

District Attorney Michael Latin

William J. Genego, Esquire (appeals attorney for Brandon Hein)

William Gazecki (creator/director/producer of *Reckless Indifference*)

Randall Sullivan (*Rolling Stone* magazine reporter)

Linda Triano (sister of Judie Farris)

Nicole Weinberg (best childhood friend of Jason Holland)

Melissa Page (girlfriend of Jason Holland)

Karen Baxter (longtime advocate for Brandon Hein and criminal justice lobbyist)

Scott Budnick (twenty-year advocate of all four defendants; lobbyist who persuaded Governor Schwarzenegger to commute Brandon Hein's sentence)

ABOUT THE AUTHOR

Since earning a degree in psychology and biology from UCLA, Eve Porinchak has lived all over the planet and spent much of her time in and out of prison—as a creative writing teacher and advocate for teen inmates. Eve serves as an aid worker in Tijuana orphanages and is an agent with Jill Corcoran Literary Agency in Los Angeles. A former medical student, child welfare social worker, and first-grade teacher, Eve writes stories featuring youths she feels have been underrepresented in children's literature, such as those born into gang life, the abandoned, the incarcerated, and war refugees, who—ironically—have the most fascinating tales to tell.

DISCOVER NEW YA READS

READ BOOKS FOR FREE

WIN NEW & UPCOMING RELEASES

RIVETED

YA FICTION **IS OUR ADDICTION**

JOIN THE COMMUNITY

DISCUSS WITH THE COMMUNITY

WRITE FOR THE COMMUNITY

CONNECT WITH US ON RIVETEDLIT.COM

AND @RIVETEDLIT